DM

CU00953167

Gurus for Government

I C S A
Publishing

in association with
LIGIC

The author

Alan Fowler's career spans the private and public sectors. After 20 years in personnel appointments in four different industries he joined the GLC as head of the industrial relations branch. He later moved to a chief officer post with Hampshire County Council, heading the combined personnel and management services function. Since 1988 he has worked as a freelance personnel consultant, mainly though not solely in local government. His clients have included the Audit Commission, South East Employers, the States of Jersey, a major Civil Service trade union and numerous UK local authorities.

He writes extensively on personnel and management topics, with a monthly column in *Local Government Chronicle* and frequent articles in *People Management*, the journal of the Institute of Personnel and Development (IPD). His books include *What Every Councillor should know about Personnel* (LGC, 1991); *Human Resource Management in Local Government* (Longman, 2nd edition 1995); *Taking Charge: A Guide to People Management in Today's Public Sector* (IPM, 1993); and a number of books published by the IPD on a variety of personnel topics.

Gurus for Government
Lessons from management gurus for local government managers

Alan Fowler

First Published 1997 by
ICSA Publishing Limited
Campus 400, Maylands Avenue
Hemel Hempstead
Hertfordshre HP2 7EZ

Printed and bound in Great Britain by
T.J. Press Ltd., Padstow, Cornwall

British Library Cataloguing in Publiction Data

A catalogue for this book is available from the British Library.

ISBN 1 8607 2040 4
Price: £24.95

Contents

Foreword

When I asked Alan to write this book it was because of his enormous writing skill and knowledge of the great management theories and of public administration.

Nobody before has attempted to extract the best ideas of these inspiring gurus and to see how they are, or could be, applied to the demanding circumstances of managing local authorities and other public organisations.

Fortunately for the future of the public sector, the answer is that these great ideas can indeed be used by managers. But Alan shows how this can only be done by acting with intelligence and thoughtful understanding.

He has achieved this with a combination of critical analysis, penetrating dissection and dazzling style that reminded me why he still writes regularly for *LGC* despite two changes of editor since I first offered him a column in 1980.

Alan has knowledge, wisdom, wit and can spot and de-bunk a posturing buffoon a mile-off. In this book he does the lot.

Crispin Derby
LGC Communications

Preface

It is sometimes as important to explain what a book is not, as it is to highlight its intentions. So for the avoidance of doubt, as the lawyers say, let me make clear that this book is neither a comprehensive and unbiased summary of what the gurus say, nor is it about government per se. It is a personal selection of topics and gurus which I have found interesting, enlightening or occasionally infuriating, together with my personal and no doubt biased views about the applicability of the ideas concerned to the management of local authorities.

It is focused specifically on management gurus and management concepts and techniques – not on the ideas of academics and others about the nature or structure of government. I am very happy to leave that field to those two leading UK commentators, Professors John Stewart and George Jones. Consequently, there is very little reference in this book to such topics as elected mayors, subsidiarity or community governance – fascinating and important though these ideas may be.

If I had wanted to write about different concepts of local government, I would probably have been diverted into a discussion of the fascinating upside-down nature of the governmental structure in Switzerland, where real power rests primarily with the 3,000 communes and 26 cantons; and where 50,000 citizens' signatures can requisition a national referendum. Or I might have devoted a chapter to a location with a population of only 80,000 which has a single governmental tier running everything from hospitals, prisons and schools to electricity generation, an airport and harbours, with all the other national and local government services in between – the States of Jersey. But all that would have been a very different book.

Here, the subject is management and the extent to which the ideas of the management gurus can help or hinder. On this, I confess to having a somewhat schizophrenic approach. On the one hand, I like to set the practicalities of management within the broader conceptual context which many gurus write about. On the other hand, I am deeply suspicious of any guru's claim that his or her theory holds the key to organisational success. Some managers' uncritical enthusiasm for the latest management buzzword – empowerment, re-engineering or whatever –

immediately generates my determination to find flaws in the argument. I make no attempt to conceal this attitude in this book. Indeed, it would be disappointing if at least some readers did not disagree strongly with my comments on some of the gurus. Even if all the gurus do is stimulate argument they serve a useful purpose by encouraging consideration of the underlying principles and purposes of effective management. It is the unthinking acceptance either of the status quo or of management fads which is the real danger – not intelligent disagreements about either the answers to managerial problems or, probably more constructively, the right questions.

Alan Fowler
February 1997

Chapter 1

The guru phenomenon

Anyone in the early 1950s who had asked in a bookshop for publications about management would either have drawn a blank or been directed to a very small shelf. A similar enquiry in any large bookshop today will result in the customer being shown a whole section of shelving stocked with literally hundreds of titles. Even station bookstalls now carry displays of the most popular management texts, including some which have reached best-seller status and others which claim to provide the keys to managerial success within a few minutes of light reading. The term 'management guru' has become widely used, and although there is no agreed definition of the term, three primary criteria can be suggested for recognition as one of today's gurus:

- The production of original ideas and insights into the nature and management of organisations.
- The authorship of books about these views which are widely read by managers, not just by academics and theorists, and which influence managers' understanding and activities.
- The ability to communicate their ideas and inspire managerial audiences in person, through lectures, television and videos, not only through books.

How has this guru phenomenon developed? How did it start? And how relevant to UK local government is the welter of sometimes conflicting advice from today's and yesterday's gurus, many of whom direct their messages to American business enterprises?

Management publications in the early 1950s

Go back to the bookshop of the 1950s. A secondhand section then might have had copies of perhaps the only pre-war books with the word management in their titles – FJ Roethlisberger's *Management and the Worker*, which described Elton Mayo's ground-breaking research in the period 1927 to 1932 into motivation and group behaviour in the Hawthorne Western Electric factory in the USA; and FW Taylor's earlier 1911 book, *Principles of Scientific Management* (with a first UK edition in 1947). Three books from the last three years of the 1940s might still have been in print. Chester Barnard, chief executive of the Bell Telephone Company, had written *Organization and Management* in 1948, emphasising the importance of managerial leadership, effective employee communications and company values. An English translation of *General and Industrial Management* by Henri Fayol, a French engineering manager, was published in 1949. It described fourteen 'general principles of management', including specialisation of skills, clear lines of executive authority, fair employment practices, security of tenure and *esprit de corps*. Colonel Urwick, founder of Britain's first management consultancy, Urwick Orr and Partners, authored the 1946 volume *The Making of Scientific Management*, which was largely based on Taylor's ideas.

If the bookshop enquiry had been made in 1954, the small management section might have given pride of place to a newly published book, *The Practice of Management*, by Peter Drucker. This emphasised management by objectives as the first of management's essential tasks and established Drucker as the leading management thinker of the post war years – and probably the first to be thought of as a management guru. By the 1990s, and some 20 books later, Drucker has become recognised as the thinker whose ideas about management anticipated those of almost all the many gurus of the last half of the 20th century. In 1970, the Conservative Party was also to credit Drucker with the original concept of privatisation, although in his 1969 book, *The Age of Discontinuity*, he actually used the term reprivatisation – pointing out that historically, many of the State-run activities of the 19th and 20th centuries originated with private or non-State initiatives.

Although our 1950s bookshop customer may have found only this handful of titles dealing specifically with management, a knowledgeable shop assistant might have suggested looking at other publications under the headings of sociology, social psychology or economics. Elton Mayo (of the Hawthorne research) had written two books on the human and social problems of an industrial civilisation. In the UK in 1951, Elliott Jacques wrote up the results of several years sociological research at the Glacier Metal company under the title, *The Changing Culture of a Factory* – one of the first texts to develop the concept of organisational culture. For the public sector, the most important book, though not an easy read, was the German sociologist Max Weber's *Theory of Social and Economic Organisation*. This was first published in English translation in 1947 although Weber had died in 1920. The book argued that bureaucracy was the most efficient form of organisational administration, with echoes of Alexander Pope's somewhat cynical lines of 1734:

"For forms of government let fools contest,
   Whate'er is best administered is best".

One much earlier book might also have been available in one of its many reprints since its first publication in 1776 – Adam Smith's *Wealth of Nations*. This opens with a very practical example of what was to become a dominant feature of the way almost all organisations would structure work and jobs – the division (or specialisation) of labour.

Although none of the authors before Drucker fully meets the definitional criteria of guru, much of their work either forms a basis for more recent management concepts or can be seen still to influence organisational structures and management attitudes. Three authors merit particular attention – Weber for his theory of bureaucracy, Adam Smith for the concept of the division of labour and Taylor for his principles of scientific management.

Bureaucracy

Although the terms bureaucracy and bureaucratic have become synonymous with inefficiency and red tape, it is worthwhile looking back at Weber's arguments. Some of the characteristics of bureaucracy as he described them are still relevant today as some of the best aspects of the public service ethos. Bureaucracy is not all bad.

Weber discussed alternative forms of control within organisations and contrasted bureaucracy, as a rational and legally defined system, with the alternatives of charismatic or traditional authority. The charismatic form relied solely on the personality of the current leader; the traditional or hereditary form followed historic custom and precedent. He saw the first as unpredictable and unstable, and the second as inflexible and liable to failure to adapt to changing circumstances.

A few local authorities have experienced the effects of domination by one powerful personality, though whether leaders such as Dame Shirley Porter at the City of Westminster should be described as charismatic is a matter of opinion. This type of control does, however, illustrate Weber's criticism of the organisation whose actions are over-dependent on the wishes and whims of a single individual. It is a point which needs to be considered in relation to proposals for elected mayors with executive authority. Would there then be a risk of abuses of power by dominant personalities? Would the erosion of the traditional (and bureaucratic) separation of the administration from the executive prejudice the current emphasis on the political neutrality of public servants? Might changes in leadership result in too radical changes of style and service, and unacceptable differences in service provision between local authorities?

Traditional authority is more clearly seen in a family firm in which the management passes from one generation to the next than in local government. But on a more general basis, a culture of keeping things unchanged simply because that is how they have always been done, and recruiting managers who are clones of their predecessors, comes close to Weber's concept of the traditional organisation and has certainly not been unknown in the public sector.

Weber advocated the alternative of a rational, bureaucratic system with the following features:

- Authority derives from the position and formally prescribed role of the office (the job), not from the personality of the office-holder. In other words, authority is impersonal and consistent. In public sector organisations, citizens experience the same response from the same office, regardless of who the office-holder happens to be.

- There is a rational and legally defined hierarchy of offices, with each office-holder's duties set out in writing, with clear lines of accountability and authority. Work is undertaken in accordance with written and standardised rules and procedures.
- Office-holders are appointed and promoted on merit and for their relevant expertise. Where possible, selection is by examination or by the possession of relevant formal qualifications.
- Office-holders are subject to strict requirements regarding their conduct, but cannot be lightly dismissed.
- Office-holders (as administrators) are separate from the owners or political leaders of the organisation, and are thus politically neutral.
- There is a total absence of nepotism and corruption, and a clear separation of official duties from personal interests or obligations.
- Salaries are related to the status and responsibility of the job.

Weber saw the bureaucratic organisation as a smoothly running machine and claimed that the advantages of such a system included precision, an absence of ambiguity, continuity, reliability, consistency, efficiency and probity.

It is obvious that until recently, local authorities as well as the Civil Service, have operated very closely in accordance with all these principles. It is equally clear that the criticisms of bureaucracy which have led to a fundamental questioning of Weber's ideas have resulted from in-built flaws or tendencies in the bureaucratic system. Some of these potential flaws had been identified during Weber's lifetime, with the German sociologist Robert Michels pointing to the tendency of bureaucracies to preserve their own power and, in his words, to cease being a tool and become a master. The concept of the organisation as a machine clearly carries the possibility that the organisation's style and activities will become mechanistic. Other failings include an obsession with rules and regulations, the stifling of initiative and imagination, over-complex hierarchies, compliance with detailed procedures becoming an end in itself, impersonality being taken to the point of insensitivity and just too much paperwork.

While it is easy to list bureaucratic failings, it would be regrettable if this led to the loss of the principal beneficial characteristics of bureaucracy, which include:

- High standards of probity and conduct.
- Clarity of legal rights and obligations.
- The political neutrality of officers.
- Consistency of service standards.
- Efficient administrative processes.
- High standards of professional expertise.
- Officers appointed and paid on merit.

Current developments, such as extensive organisational devolution, the disbanding of detailed procedure manuals, the internal market and commercialisation, pose a serious challenge to some of these qualities. For example, if decision-making powers within a local authority are devolved extensively to the managers and staff of dozens of largely autonomous business units, will citizens experience the same qualities and standards of service across all the authority's functions? And if these same managers are expected to produce commercial results in a market-oriented culture, what non-bureaucratic safeguards will there be to prevent a slippage of standards of conduct and probity?

The currently fashionable denigration of administration and professionalism in favour of management also has dangers. Accurate records, the effective control and analysis of financial transactions, efficient procedures for citizens to apply for access to services, keeping track of service usage – these are all necessary activities requiring the design and operation of efficient administrative processes. Many local government services also require the input of a high level of professional expertise if quality and efficiency are to be maintained. Some professionals can certainly be faulted for acting as though promoting the status of their own profession takes priority over the delivery of high quality services and the convenience of citizens. But to downgrade professional excellence in favour of what is often little more than a vaguely perceived concept of all-purpose management may damage service quality for the sake of following managerial fashion. And followers of fashion who highlight the key role of management should also note that whereas administrators and professionals have until recently been criticised for not being managers, managers are now being similarly criticised for not being leaders – a point discussed in more detail in chapter 11. Keeping up with the gurus can be a stressful occupation.

These comments are not a plea for retaining the entire structure and style of the local authority of the pre-1990s. Complex hierarchies, insensitive procedures, an over-reliance on the rule book, in-fighting for influence between different departments or professions – these are all tendencies which the bureaucratic organisation can too readily develop. But in implementing corrective measures there is a danger of disbanding the checks, balances and values which are, or should be, specific to public sector bodies with their unique accountability to citizens and communities. The challenge is to safeguard the good features of bureaucracy within the less rigid, more adaptable and innovative organisational culture which current gurus advocate and most authorities are trying to evolve.

Division of labour

There are many remarkable features about Adam Smith's famous book, *The Wealth of Nations* – particularly when it is remembered that it preceded the Industrial Revolution. It is best known for the argument that a combination of self-interest and competition within a free market is the key to economic prosperity and a stable society. Or as he put it: "Self-seeking men are often led by an invisible hand, without their knowing it, to advance the interest of society". But the book opens with an account of how 10 persons, properly equipped and working as a team and with each handling just one part of the whole process, could produce 48,000 pins each day. One person working alone and by hand, said Smith, might be unable to make more than one pin in a day.

This simple example, used by Smith to illustrate the benefits of a combination of labour and capital, was the precursor of the whole concept of the division of labour – in all kinds of work, not just in manual operations. It is a concept which tends to be taken for granted because it is the way all large organisations have structured their activities. The total work involved in any major process is broken down into a series of tasks, each of which becomes a job. Performing the tasks in the right sequence produces the desired end result. The argument is that a combination of job specialisation supported by the necessary equipment or technology achieves much higher productivity and consistency of quality than if individual workers had to handle the entire process.

While the most obvious applications of this concept can be seen in the manufacturing industry – the car factory or Adam Smith's pin workshop – the principle has also been a major influence on the way much white collar work is organised. For example, a social services office receives a request for the home help service. A clerk logs the request and issues an acknowledgement and a form requesting more details. These documents are passed to the postroom where another clerk processes their despatch. On receipt of the application form (again logged by a clerk) it is passed to an administrator for preliminary assessment of eligibility and cost. If it passes this hurdle, details are passed to a home help supervisor to make an initial visit to decide the frequency of help and the charges to be made. Copies of the agreed arrangements are passed to the designated home help, the area office and the finance department – where another clerk starts the necessary charging procedure. From the first request to a home help actually starting work, at least five people will be involved. The technological support for this division of tasks is not so obvious as the high-cost machinery in a factory process, but telephones, word-processing and computerised records are probably all essential.

The concept of the division of labour was developed in the scientific management movement which is discussed in more detail below. Here, two points are worth noting:

- There is no inevitability in the way a whole process is divided into tasks and jobs and the current pattern may no longer be appropriate. Because of the integral link between technology and the design of work, and because of the speed of development of information and communication technology, the design options for the way work and jobs are structured are now very wide and varied.
- Although Adam Smith used his example to illustrate the economic benefits of job specialisation, he also commented that simple, highly repetitive work could result in the intellectual degradation of the worker. In redesigning the way work is sequenced and divided into separate jobs, the human dimension needs as much consideration as the technical or administrative aspects.

Scientific management

In 1947, 135 years after *The Wealth of Nations*, FW Taylor's seminal book, *Scientific Management* was published. Taylor, an American engineer, was an efficiency nut. He was obsessed by the idea that there must be one best way of doing any particular task, a view which as a college student led him to invent overarm pitching at baseball as more effective than the then standard underarm delivery. Later, as an engineer and consultant, he argued that by detailed observation and analysis of work of all kinds – managerial as well as administrative and manual – it was possible to identify the single most efficient method of working and to define how long each element in this method should take. Linked to this analytical approach were five other principles:

- Work was best divided into small units in order to minimise the amount of skill needed and allow maximum specialisation.
- Workers should be set quantified daily work quotas.
- Workers should be motivated by financial incentives linked to performance.
- Work should be subject to close supervision and inspection.
- Work should be organised to ensure the most efficient flow of materials and sequence of tasks.

Taylor's emphasis on dividing work into small units had been advocated at about the same time by Henri Fayol, the French engineer referred to briefly earlier in this chapter. The first of Fayol's 14 general management principles was work specialisation, or as he put it: "The object of the division of work is to produce more and better work with the same effort". For Taylor, chopping work processes into the smallest practicable pieces also facilitated detailed work analysis and measurement, and his ideas triggered the invention of work study (then generally termed time and motion study) and O&M (organisation and methods).

Work study was adopted enthusiastically by American industry, while ICI took a lead in its use in the UK. (Sir John Harvey-Jones originally joined ICI as a work study officer.) The British Civil Service developed O&M for the review and improvement of white collar work, and UK local authorities began to make extensive use of both techniques in the 1950s and 1960s.

Taylor and Fayol, copied by Urwick, extended their thinking beyond the individual worker to the organisation as a whole, and promoted the concept of the functional division of an organisation's corporate activities. Taylor actually used the phrase 'functional management' to describe the establishment of separate departments for design, finance, purchasing, production and sales. Fayol emphasised the role of senior management in ensuring the coordination of these separate functions. Urwick, no doubt influenced by his Army experience, developed the concept of 'line and staff' in which functions such as finance and personnel were seen as providing staff support to line managers – the generalists who had executive and coordinating authority. Local authority finance staff who do not like their role being described simply as a support service should blame Colonel Urwick.

It is difficult to over estimate the powerful and often damaging influence of 'Taylorism' in its various guises on managerial attitudes and assumptions, and on the way most large organisations, private and public, have been structured. Departmentalism in local authorities, now coming under increasing criticism for its failure to deal effectively with issues which cross traditional service boundaries, is one example. The inflexibility of very detailed job descriptions is another. Work

study, once seen as the answer to efficiency in manual work such as grounds maintenance, has already been largely discredited, particularly for the way in which
work-studied incentive schemes decay into expensive payment systems. Doubts are
growing about the effectiveness of performance-related pay in other types of work.

Yet the concept still has an intellectual attraction for many managers because of
its pseudo-scientific logic and rationality. To the logical mind, there must surely be
'one best way'. To the orderly mind, there must be advantages in everything from the
macro structure of the organisation to the minutiae of each job being clearly defined.
Because a well-designed machine runs smoothly and sweetly, the closer an organisation can be made to operate like a machine, the more efficient and effective it is likely
to be. And the fact that people can be illogical, awkward or inconsistent only adds
emphasis, in the mind of the scientific manager, to the need for the unquestioned
compliance with closely prescribed job roles, methods and procedures.

This last point highlights the hugely important missing factor in Taylor's scientific management theory – the real impact and implications of the human factor.
Fayol recognised this to some extent by including in his 14 management principles
the need to maintain a sense of *esprit de corps*. In practice, however, the 'soft'
human factors have generally rated a lower priority than the 'hard' and more readily
definable structural and procedural matters. Any objectives relating to morale and
motivation have also been thought by too many managers to be met simply by the
provision of financial incentives – or in the case of public sector bodies by providing
security of tenure and a Buggins' turn system of career progression.

That said, some aspects of the so-called scientific approach still have practical
relevance. Peter Drucker has pointed out that Taylor was a pioneer in terms of
studying the nature of work – and while the conclusions to be made from such
studies today differ from Taylor's, the practice of analysing what works well and
less well, and why, is still vitally important to the design of effective organisational
structures and systems. There are also still many processes which, for reasons of
consistency, public accountability or the law, require definitions of method, and
compliance with prescribed procedures. One example is the process of taking a
vulnerable child into care – a far too serious and sensitive issue to be left to the
personal decision of a single 'empowered' employee. Other examples, in the employment field, are the formal procedures for handling discipline and redundancy,
without which an employer risks being found unfair when a dismissal is challenged
in an Industrial Tribunal. Most authorities, too, have found it important to introduce documented complaints procedures to ensure consistency of response, while
strictly enforced health and safety rules are often essential. Local authorities are
certainly not machines, and employees are not mere units of production, but there
is still a need for a robust framework of structure and system within which
employees, teams and managers can exercise their initiative and imagination.

From the 1950s to today: human resource management

Specific theories and views of the growing number of management gurus over
the past four decades, and the relevance of these ideas to local authorities, are

discussed in the next 10 chapters. It may be helpful, however, to set some of these developments in the context of two broad and related themes about the management of people – the human relations movement of the 1960s and its current successor, human resource management.

As noted earlier, despite the attractions to many managers of the systematic, rational but mechanistic approach of scientific management, theorists and some managers quickly recognised its failure to take effective account of the realities and complexities of the human factor. Taylor's theories implied that employees were inherently lazy, indifferent to the needs of their employing organisations, uninterested in doing a good job, and motivated primarily by money. The managerial response therefore needed to be a mix of carrot and stick. Even before the 2nd World War this view had been challenged. Elton Mayo had discovered from his Hawthorne experiments that factors such as recognition and group morale had a major influence on employees' performance. Fayol, too, accepted the reality of the morale factor. Mary Parker Follet (an American political scientist) expounded the view that in a democracy, the task for managements is to create a working environment in which people willingly give of their best. She also emphasised the importance of team-working.

Curiously, Follet (together with Deming, the quality guru) was accorded far more recognition and respect in immediate post-war Japan than in the USA or the UK, and it was not until the 1960s that many Western managements took serious notice of the importance of the human factor. Much of this burgeoning interest was triggered by the American social psychologist, Douglas Macgregor, and his 1960 book *The Human Side of Enterprise*. This labelled the Taylor concept Theory X and his own opposite view, Theory Y. Theory Y assumed that employees essentially want to do a good job, that they respond to being treated as intelligent adults, and that factors such as interesting work and personal recognition are more powerful motivators than money. (Motivation is considered in more detail in chapter 6.)

The consequence was the emergence of what became known as the 'human relations' approach to management, with a particular emphasis on creating satisfying jobs, developing joint consultative processes, more extensive training, improving employee communications, studying group dynamics, and training supervisors to be better managers of people. In the private sector, this resulted in a rapid expansion of the personnel function, though in local government in the 1960s, the bureaucratic approach of the establishment officer continued to dominate. Few local authorities apart from the Greater London Council recruited professionally qualified personnel officers prior to the 1974 reorganisation.

Both the private and public sectors experienced disappointment with the human relations approach during the late 1970s as a result of an upsurge in confrontational industrial relations. Some political commentators pointed out that in emphasising the importance of the attitudes of individual employees and small groups, and in its assumption that employees and employers shared common goals, the approach failed to address the wider collective interest of employees as trade union members and what was often an underlying conflict of interest between shareholders, management and workers. Be that as it may, the fact is that managing industrial relations tended to dominate management thinking at this time. Experiences in local government such as the fire service strike of 1977 and the 'winter of discontent' of 1978/79 were not, to put it mildly, conducive to the development of the warm, friendly approach to employee management which the human relations school advocated. In the private sector, the term 'macho management' began to be used to describe the much harsher and Taylorite attitude which industrial action and the new Conservative government's anti-union stance tended to encourage.

In the early 1980s, the term 'human resource management' (soon shortened to HRM) emerged in the USA to mark a shift of thinking about the management of people. Unlike many management terms or buzzwords which have originated with a single author, it is difficult to pin HRM on any single guru, though much of the original literature about the concept came from the Harvard Business School. The extent to which HRM represents a genuinely new or different approach has also been confused by the words 'human resources' being widely substituted for 'personnel' in many circumstances in which nothing has changed except the terminology. This is particularly true of job titles, where Directors of Human Resources are beginning to outnumber Directors of Personnel. It is unlikely that this represents a dramatic change in the nature of many of these managers' work.

So is HRM just a fancy term for personnel management? In some cases it is, but as a concept, HRM has some specific features which differ significantly from the conventional personnel bias towards the human relations approach. Indeed, it was the perceived failure of human relations theories which led Harvard to develop HRM. The two major weaknesses of the way human relations theory had been applied in practice were seen as:

- Treating personnel management as separate or additional to the central business activity, instead of it being an integral part of effective business management.
- As a corollary, leaving many personnel functions to be undertaken by personnel specialists, thus encouraging line managers to abdicate their responsibility for the effective management of their people.

The three most positive principles of HRM, as expounded by a variety of academics and consultants, are:

- Human resource issues and strategies should be considered within the whole business planning activity and not dealt with after business strategies have been determined.
- Managers should accept that the effective management of people is a central line management function which should not be devolved to personnel specialists.
- An organisation's people are its most important asset. Employees should be seen as a resource – a form of capital – and not simply as a revenue cost.

These ideas, if accepted, carry several important implications for local authorities.

It has been a common practice for managers to develop proposals for service policies, and for elected members to agree these proposals, without taking full account of the human resource implications. For example, a county council's social services committee endorsed a plan to double the scale of the occupational therapy service within a year. It soon became evident that because of a national shortage of qualified occupational therapists, this objective was unrealistic. An HRM approach would have ensured that the recruitment practicalities were taken into account before the policy was endorsed – not afterwards. With the practice of business planning being adopted by many authorities and encouraged by the Audit Commission, HRM principles require that factors such as recruitment and training form an integral part of any business plan.

On the second of the three principles, many authorities have already devolved responsibility for a number of employment activities from personnel specialists to line and unit managers. Managers now make decisions about recruitment, promotion, training and payments which in the past have been left to the personnel function. It is difficult to fault the theory of this type of devolution. Really effective managers need to have the authority to make decisions about who they employ and how they should be trained and rewarded. But for many managers – particularly those whose primary interest is in the technical or operational aspects of their unit's work – these new responsibilities can be very onerous and may not be handled at all skilfully. In theory, the HRM approach should be very effective. Introduced with inadequate planning or support, the practice can be considerably less satisfactory than what went before.

There are therefore three preconditions to successful devolution of personnel management to line managers:

- The authority should define the values and standards of employee management which it wishes to see implemented by all managers across all services.
- Managers should be given training to enable them to take on their new responsibilities effectively.
- A professional personnel function should be retained, partly to contribute to strategic thinking in the corporate core, partly to be available as a point of specialist information and advice to managers at large.

Treating people as a resource and not a cost sounds fine in theory but is difficult to reconcile with the parallel development in the wider use of temporary staff, fixed term contracts and redundancy programmes. Cynical employees will interpret management's grand HRM statements as: "People are our most important asset, and we intend to employ as few of them as possible". However, if over-hyped statements can be avoided, the concept of people as a resource does have important and valuable implications. In particular:

- It encourages managers to draw on the ideas and expertise which exists among employees at all levels, and especially from those in the front line.
- It highlights the importance of training as a form of investment in the development of a highly competent and committed workforce.

Learning from the gurus

How should local authority managers make best use of the stream of views and advice which today fills the bookshelves and management journals? One reaction is largely to ignore the management literature on the somewhat cynical grounds, either that it is all just common sense dressed up in jargon; or that if one waits a year or two, every new idea is shown to have been no more than a passing fashion.

Anyone with a heavy daily workload will have some sympathy with this attitude, but it is one which runs serious risks of becoming stuck in an intellectual rut, carrying on with management practices which are ineffective, and in career terms falling behind colleagues who take continuing professional development more seriously. There are significant benefits in keeping abreast of new management thinking, subject to certain safeguards:

- Much of the guru material has originated in the USA and has been based on, or directed towards, the American private sector. In recent years, American gurus such as Rosabeth Moss Kanter have been particularly concerned with the threat to America's economic prosperity of competition from Japan and the Pacific Rim. Not all the ideas which emerge from these concerns have very obvious relevance to UK local authorities.

- Some caution is also needed in adopting management practices which may be acceptable in an American culture but which might not have the same beneficial impact in the UK. Just because Americans speak English does not mean that they have the same cultural characteristics. To take just one example, American managers as individuals are uninhibited about saying how great they are, and some gurus encourage this as a form of self confidence-boosting. Many UK managers would find this uncomfortable and unhelpful.

- Very few gurus, American, British or European, centre their ideas on the public sector. Almost all base their research and theories on private sector businesses. They may make passing references to the applicability of their ideas to the public sector and, of course, many concepts are transferable between sectors. Nevertheless, the local government reader needs to import the implications of the public service ethos and of the integral political element into their assessment of messages from the gurus.

- Some management material, too, is appropriate only for the organisation which can choose to limit its activity to a single product or service. Local authorities are multi-functional organisations which do not have a fully free choice about their range of activities.

- It is as well to be very sceptical of any guru's claim that one particular new idea provides the single key to managerial or business success. Management is far too complex a function to be susceptible to single-subject easy fixes.

- Managers should avoid the over-enthusiastic acceptance of a concept or technique simply because other organisations are adopting it. The history of management is littered with examples of unsuccessful fads and fashions.

- It is also important to consider the impact of any one new management concept on other aspects of management which the guru concerned may not have addressed. The failure in many organisations of once fashionable quality circles has been largely due to their being introduced without necessary supporting changes being made to supervisory and decision-making systems.

These warning notes may seem so extensive as to suggest that most management gurus should be ignored, but that is not the message this book is intended to convey. All that is being urged is that managers should avoid jumping on managerial bandwagons and, instead, give close and careful consideration to the new ideas which the gurus are continuously expounding. In particular, thought needs to be given to the applicability of these ideas to the institution, function and culture of UK local government – a matter on which almost all the gurus, American, European and British, are silent.

Given such consideration, there is much to be learned from many of yesterday's and today's gurus. For managers who like to set their role within a wide framework of theory or principle, some gurus can provide a helpful conceptual map or set of guidelines. For the activist manager who likes to plunge in and experiment in the context of daily activities, other gurus will suggest many new ways of handling everyday management tasks. And there are gurus who will offer the revolutionary manager fundamentally new approaches to the age-old problem of how best to organise work, manage people, and improve performance.

The remaining chapters are a personal selection of some management concepts which either have most relevance to local authorities or have generated a great deal of interest but need to be treated with caution. Readers who keep up with the management literature or attend management seminars may have other ideas. That is fine. There is no one right answer, and provided the gurus' ideas are given intelligent scrutiny, it is entirely acceptable for different managers to reach different conclusions about their validity. After all, what works for one local authority may not work for another. Other readers who perhaps have not previously paid much regard to what the gurus say may be encouraged to take more interest in future. Their starting point is probably to develop the habit of scanning the management journals, rather than embarking on an onerous book-reading list, although footnotes refer to some seminal texts and a short list of books is suggested in the appendix for further reading.

Chapter 2

The Seven Ss

McKinsey & Company has long been one of the USA's leading firms of management consultants, operating internationally and renowned for the number of its partners who have gone on to become famous figures in the worlds of business management and management education. Sir John Banham and Howard Davies, both former chairmen of the Audit Commission and directors general of the CBI, are former McKinsey consultants, although the majority of the firm's best known partners are American.

Towards the end of the 1970s, three McKinsey consultants in the States (Tom Peters, Robert Waterman, Richard Pascale) became involved in studies of American and Japanese companies in an attempt to identify the characteristics which led to business success. Their work led them to the conclusion that there were at least seven interdependent variables involved, which they first described as: structure, strategy, people, management style, systems or procedures, culture, and corporate strengths or skills. They were then advised by Antony Athos of the Harvard Business School to describe these factors by seven words beginning with the same letter – hence the eventual McKinsey 7-S Framework. (3-S, 1-P, 1-MS, 1-C and 1-CS would not have had the same ring!).

The seven Ss defined

In more detail, the seven Ss were described as:

- **Shared values:** the beliefs or concepts the company imbues in its people.
- **Strategy:** how a company plans to achieve its long term business objectives.
- **Structure:** how the company divides up (and links) its various parts.
- **Style:** the way managers behave and relate to the outside world and each other.
- **Systems:** the procedures and methods by which work is done.
- **Staff:** the human dimension; the composition and commitment of the workforce.
- **Skills:** the company's expertise.

The team had some difficulty finding a satisfactory term beginning with S for the first of these factors, originally labelling it 'superordinate goals'. This was eventually changed to 'shared values' by Richard Pascale, whose book, *The Art of Japanese Management*, compared and contrasted American and Japanese businesses in their approach to the seven Ss. He concluded that there was a tendency in the USA to concentrate on the 'hard' factors of strategy, structure and systems, whereas the most successful Japanese firms paid equal attention to the apparently 'soft' factors of style, staff and shared values. Pascale commented that what some American managers considered mere froth had "the power of the Pacific". One of his main points, too, was that shared values provide "the glue that holds the other six Ss together" – and many companies had never defined what their values were. In 1982, a year after Pascale's book, the 7-S concept achieved much wider publicity by its inclusion in the all-time management best-seller, *In Search of Excellence*, by Peters and Waterman, which is discussed in more detail in chapter 3.

Two important ideas about 7-S as developed by the American consultants, and in addition to the cohesive effect of shared values, are:

- An organisation's approach to each factor must be consistent with the approach to all the other factors.
- A change to one factor will probably require changes to some or all of the others.

So an opportunistic style needs to be matched by flexibility in strategy, structure and systems. Similarly, any new system may need adjustments to the structure, require new skills, must contribute to the success of the strategy and reflect the shared values.

The 7-S concept and local government

How relevant is the 7-S concept to UK local government? Can an idea which arose from studies of American and Japanese commercial enterprises be applied in any realistic and constructive way to British local authorities? At first sight, the massive differences in culture, role and function between the organisations studied by the McKinsey team and those managed by readers of this current book may appear too wide to permit the transfer of any managerial concepts. In reality, however, the 7-S approach can be a valuable aid to UK local authorities as a framework of principles either for use as an organisational health check or to assess the probable implications or effectiveness of any major change.

Before suggesting how the 7-S framework can be used in these ways, it is helpful to adapt the definitions of the seven factors to fit the local government scene:

- **Shared values:** the qualities which the authority believes should characterise everything it does.
- **Strategy:** the broad aims for the authority as a whole and for each service – the general direction the authority and its services are taking and how they plan to develop.
- **Structure:** how the authority divides up its various activities into committees, panels, departments, functions, units and jobs.

- **Style:** the authority's general character or organisational personality – including how members and officers behave and relate to each other.
- **Systems:** all the various processes, methods and procedures for getting work done – including corporate information and monitoring systems.
- **Staff:** how the authority manages its people; the size and constitution of the workforce.
- **Skills:** the stock of skill and know-how within the workforce; the particular skills or abilities of the authority and each service as a whole.

In using this set of factors, there are four key principles to keep in mind:

— All seven factors are important. The effective authority pays attention to every one of the seven and does not consider that some are softer or less important than others.

— There needs to be a compatibility of approach to all seven factors. For example, an informal and opportunistic style is incompatible with a rigid and highly formalised set of systems.

— If a change is made to any one factor, consideration should be given to the likelihood of complementary change being required to most or all of the others.

— Compatibility and consistency are impossible to achieve without a clear view of corporate values.

The starting point for any authority is therefore to define its values, and these should be distinguished from the rather fashionable but far less helpful 'mission statement'. Mission statements have become widely publicised in the private sector, and normally declare that the company concerned aims to be the leader in its particular field. Some councils have copied this approach and produced statements saying simply that they aim to be the best local authority in the country. There is nothing wrong with enthusiasm and ambition as such, but this type of statement is of very little assistance in guiding the authority in its decisions. What does 'best' mean? Best at what? Cutting costs? Winning CCT bids? Helping the aged?

Core values

Statements of corporate or core values are (or can be) of much more use in shaping the authority's plans and activities. They are the qualities and principles which should influence everything the authority does and how its members, managers and staff at large behave. An example drawn from one south coast council[1] illustrates how the definition and promotion of a set of values can permeate the entire authority. The authority has summarised its values as:

- Respect for the democratic process.
- Responsiveness to customers and the community.
- Partnership working with other organisations.
- Concern for the environment.
- Fairness, openness and helpfulness in internal and external relationships.
- The avoidance of extremes in relation to market principles.
- Prudence in the management and use of the council's assets.

Simply to produce such a schedule within a committee report and have it formally endorsed by the elected members can, of course, make as little real impact as an idealistic mission statement. Worse, it may be viewed with cynicism by a workforce which cannot detect any change or improvement in the way the authority is organised and managed. The word 'shared' in the 7-S element of shared values is critical. Values need to be explained, promoted and acted on by elected members and by staff at all levels if they are to be effective. The authority whose values are quoted above issued the following very practical explanation to all its staff:

"**Respect for the democratic process** means that we firmly support the principle that local authorities are led by elected representatives of local people. The councillors decide what the council should do. The staff assist the council in this role and have a duty to deliver the results elected members seek. In addition, we support councillors as individuals in their roles of representing their electors and monitoring how well services are delivered in their constituencies. This does not imply waiting to be told what to do. Councillors expect managers to initiate ideas and help to identify issues which may require formal council or committee decisions.

Responsiveness is concerned with the quality of the authority's relationships with individual users of our services and with the whole local community. It means we should continually look outwards to the needs of the borough's citizens and place our priority on meeting these needs. Internally, the same principles apply when one function or unit provides a service to another and there is therefore a provider/customer relationship.

Partnership involves working with other organisations for the good of the local community. This includes the development of links with the county and neighbouring authorities, the utilities (gas, water, rail etc.), local businesses, community groups, schools and colleges, and many special interest groups. This also has internal implications – the need for cooperative working between different functions and units.

Concern for the environment requires us to think about the impact on the environment of everything we do, try to eliminate any adverse effects, and look for opportunities for improving the quality of life in the borough.

Fairness, openness and helpfulness are qualities we should develop both in our contacts with each other and in our relationships with the public. It includes being open and honest about mistakes, sharing information, and being willing to help each other to cope with change and do things better.

Avoidance of extremes in market principles means that the council takes a balanced view of whether an activity is undertaken in-house or bought-in from an external provider. We seek neither to keep activities in-house at any cost nor to buy in services for the sake of buying-in. The test is effectiveness and value for money – not any pro- or anti- market dogma.

Prudence in the management and use of the council's assets is a value which recognises that managers and staff do not own the council's property and finances. We have to manage them carefully on behalf of elected members and the public. We should all try to avoid any form of waste and take great care of whatever council assets we are entrusted with".

Other authorities might well give a different emphasis to some of the values in this example, or include other factors such as equality of opportunity, the achievement of the lowest possible tax rates, or economic prosperity. The important point is not so much what the various values are, but that values have been defined and promoted. Once this has been done, the schedule of values provides a set of guiding principles which should influence everything the authority does and how everyone behaves.

Suppose, for example, that a director of leisure services begins to develop ideas for a more intensive use of the authority's recreation grounds. Using the example quoted earlier, these ideas can be checked for the extent to which they are consistent with the authority's values. Questions triggered by each of the values might include:

- **Respect for the democratic process:** will the ideas be developed with the full involvement and support of the elected members? (It is not unknown for officers with strong personal or professional preferences to attempt to achieve their objectives by manipulating or even bypassing the democratic procedures.)
- **Responsiveness to customers and the community:** is there evidence that the ideas reflect the real needs and wishes of local people? Or is the director making untested assumptions about what people want?
- **Partnership working:** would there be possibilities and advantages in developing the ideas in association with other organisations, such as local sports clubs and community groups? (There are still some professional officers who seem to feel it is a weakness to bring in 'outsiders'; or who lack the confidence to involve external interest groups in case control is lost).
- **Concern for the environment:** what would be the environmental effect of the proposed new uses for the recreation grounds? Might a balance need to be struck between, say, the financial benefits of increased revenue from new facilities and some loss of open-space amenity?
- **Fairness, openness and helpfulness:** are the ideas being discussed and developed honestly and openly with all those concerned? Or are potentially adverse factors being concealed and potential opponents kept in the dark?
- **Avoiding market extremes:** in considering how the proposed new facilities might be operated, is a balanced view being taken of the pros and cons of using in-house or external providers?

- **Prudence in the use of the council's assets:** what are the potential financial risks and benefits of the proposals? Might the degree of risk be unacceptable without additional safeguards?

The 7-S framework as a checklist

The whole 7-S framework can be used in a similar way as a checklist, particularly to ensure that changes being made to one are reviewed for their effect on the other factors. Suppose, for example, that in the previous example it is decided to introduce a new range of leisure activities in the council's recreation grounds. The 7-S framework would then suggest the following questions:

- Would the general characteristics of the proposed new facilities and how they would be publicised and operated be consistent with the council's **values**?
- Is the initiative in accord with the council's overall **strategy** for leisure services? Does the strategy include maximising the active utilisation of the council's open spaces and, if not, does such a strategy now need to be discussed and defined?
- Will the **style** of the management of the new facilities be in accordance with the style or character which the authority wishes to establish across all its services? For example, if the targeted style is informal and flexible, access to and control of the new facilities should reflect these characteristics.
- How will the new facilities be fitted into the authority's organisation **structure**? Can this be accommodated within existing units or will a new section or management position be needed?
- What new **systems** will be needed to control access to, charging for, or monitoring of, the new facilities?
- What **staff** will be required, how should they best be deployed, how might they be encouraged to contribute their ideas to the running of the new facilities, what should their objectives be?
- Are any new **skills** involved in the operation and management of the facilities? If so, how are these to be obtained or developed?

The interaction, in particular, between structure, systems, style and skills is one to which not all authorities pay sufficient attention. There has been a marked tendency in recent years to concentrate on structural change almost to the exclusion of other factors. An example might be an otherwise rather traditional authority which follows the fashionable organisational trend of reducing its number of directors to two or three multi-functional posts, with the next tier consisting of, say, 20 unit managers. It does this in line with a strategy of achieving a flatter management structure and with the aim of saving money on salaries at chief officer level. The theory is that the very small team of directors is free to concentrate on strategic issues, while the unit managers get on with operational management. But simply making this change to the organisation structure will achieve little unless changes are made to decision-making systems and it is recognised that old-style, top-down management is no longer appropriate. New skills will also be needed. Without this attention to more of 7-S than just the structure, unit managers will be frustrated by the senior directors' continued requirement to approve any operational decisions of any consequence and the directors will fail to free themselves of operational detail. In the absence of additional management training, some unit managers, too, may fail to respond effectively to their new and broader executive responsibilities.

Similar problems have arisen in some authorities which have gone down the route of introducing a hard structural split between the in-house client and contractor roles. The structural change has been implemented by the division of previously single functions into separate purchaser and provider units, but this has not been matched by supportive action in the fields of systems, style, staff or skills. A confrontational style has been allowed to develop between purchaser and provider, exacerbated by poorly defined new administrative and decision-making systems. Staff have not been involved in planning or implementing the changes and are consequently cynical or even antagonistic to the changes. Client-side managers have not had adequate training in the skills of managing through contracts: the contractor (provider) unit managers have not been helped to develop the necessary business unit skills of costing, charging and marketing their services. A 7-S approach would have identified these needs and built the necessary action into the implementation programme.

One area where there has sometimes been an obsession with system to the exclusion of other elements of 7-S has been information technology (IT). Computer enthusiasts have sold the benefits of major changes to systems without consideration for the potential impact of new systems on style, staff or skills, and not always in line with shared values or strategy. Computerising housing benefits or, say, the way applications for street parking permits are processed, may unintentionally create a different and perhaps less satisfactory style of supervision and management. New IT systems may also be ineffective unless other systems such as costing or commissioning are changed. They may be badly operated unless staff are fully informed and involved and unless adequate training is provided. They may affect the public image of the authority and clash with values such as friendliness or equality. This is not an argument against IT – IT can be designed to serve almost any value or targeted style. But if the systems element is allowed to dictate the outcome, the results may be far less satisfactory than if a holistic 7-S approach had been adopted.

Of itself, the 7-S framework will not, of course, guarantee successful change. It provides no guidance about what any change should consist of. It does not indicate the best course of action in any circumstance or set out any new management systems or techniques. It provides questions, not answers. But having a checklist of key questions is a very valuable start to the planning of any significant change, while a review of the nature of any authority's present seven Ss may reveal inconsistencies which merit correction. For example, how many authorities which claim to have adopted a friendly and informal style are fully confident that their systems and relationships with the public (and with one another, so far as members, managers and staff are concerned) reflect this style?

According to the gurus, to make the best use of the 7-S concept, it is not enough to mount a one-off review, or to use the checklist only when planning major change. Pascale's study of successful companies such as Honda convinced him that they built concern for 7-S – and for the interaction and sometimes tension between these factors – into a continuous process of debate and organisational renewal. His thesis that success breeds failure emphasised the danger of complacency and of allowing satisfactory past patterns of activity to continue past their point of relevance. But those local authorities which have built 7-S thinking into their everyday management culture would seem to be at far less risk of failure than those which either coast along on the basis of what has worked well in the past, or which introduce change on an uncoordinated basis without realising that altering one element in the way they do things will almost certainly impact on other aspects.

Footnotes:
1. Fareham Borough Council's internal staff discussion document, *Towards 2000*.

Chapter 3

The concept of excellence

With hindsight it may seem odd that the concept of organisational or company excellence did not emerge as a central feature of management literature until as recently as 1982 when Tom Peters and Robert Waterman's book, *In Search of Excellence,* was published. Prior to this, various gurus had focused attention on factors which contributed to business success, but in the main each guru addressed some specific aspect of organisation or management, rather than attempting an analysis of the totality of characteristics of the successful company.

Business success factors

Chester Barnard (an American guru who was also an industrial chief executive) had emphasised the importance of company values, a coherent company culture, and the contribution of a loyal and committed workforce to the achievement of clearly defined company goals. His ideas had a somewhat limited impact, partly because of his almost impenetrable writing style. In the 1960s, Tom Burns (a British sociologist) anticipated much of the 1990s thinking about the value of organisational flexibility by advocating 'the organic organisation' with its internal networks, team-working and shared vision. Several gurus concentrated their attention on leadership as the key to company success, typified by Rensis Likert's research into supervisory and managerial styles in American industry. He concluded that in the most successful companies, managers adopted a participative style which involved employees in the decision-making process; and that high-performing supervisors saw their primary role as the motivation of their staff – 'employee-centred' rather than 'job-centred' as Rensis put it.

The exception to gurus who each concentrated on specific aspects of successful management or successful businesses is the American guru extrordinaire, Peter Drucker. He was born in Vienna in 1909 but emigrated to the USA and soon became established as a leading academic in business studies. His first book was published in 1946, to be followed by over 20 more between then and 1990, plus hundreds of articles in the business and academic press. Still writing and lecturing in 1996, Drucker's work has prefigured almost every management concept and theory which has later been developed by other gurus. In terms of anticipating Peters and Waterman's analysis of the characteristics of excellent companies, Drucker had earlier emphasised a whole range of relevant factors – particularly the need to achieve customer satisfaction, the idea that structure should follow strategy, the importance of working towards defined goals, and the role of the manager in setting objectives, organising work, motivating and developing employees and measuring results. The problem with Drucker for the busy manager is that it is necessary to read all his books to obtain a clear picture of his overall view of organisational excellence.

A major reason for the commercial success of *In Search of Excellence* (ISOE) was that it packed a comprehensive analysis of what the authors considered to be every aspect of organisational success into one very readable volume. ISOE was based on a study by Peters and Waterman, then both McKinsey consultants, which their company began in 1977 with the aim of identifying the criteria for business success. They had first to decide what constituted a successful company and although choosing some of the firms they studied on a subjective basis, they used six statistical indices to make their final selection. These were: asset growth, equity growth, the ratio of market value to book value, and returns on capital, equity and sales.

In Search of Excellence

In considering the relevance of ISOE to UK local authorities, it is important to recognise that these statistical indices apply only to private sector enterprises. They cannot be used to identify success in the public sector. It is also interesting that the public sector and certain types of commercial organisation were excluded from the study. Financial institutions were not studied, said the authors, "because they were thought to be too highly regulated and protected to be of interest". Might not the same view be taken of local authorities, which in the UK are subject to far more regulation than banks or insurance companies? The study also ignored small companies, defined as those with an annual turnover of under $1 billion, so excluding firms of the size of district councils. It is clear that the organisations the McKinsey team were interested in were very large companies which had full freedom to decide what business they were in and how that business should be developed. So neither the selection criteria of the organisations for the study nor the criteria for organisational success can be applied to UK local authorities.

Does this mean that the ideas set out in ISOE have no relevance to councils? There are several reasons for thinking otherwise and suggesting that a discussion of the book's eight criteria for excellence is a worthwhile exercise. A very general point is that the underlying concept of comparing the characteristics of one's own organisation with those of successful comparators is very much the theme of the mid-1990s practice of benchmarking. The benchmarks which are relevant in UK local authorities may be very different from the six commercial indicators used by Peters and Waterman, but the idea of making benchmarked comparisons has become increasingly recognised as a potentially valuable aid to achieving organisational improvement. ISOE encouraged organisations to compare themselves with the best and to target excellence. In the UK, this approach underpins national initiatives such as Investors in People and Chartermark, while the Audit Commission bases many of its recommendations on its view of what constitutes excellent local authority performance.

More directly, some constructive ideas which are applicable to local authorities can be developed from most of the eight attributes of excellence. As with 7-S (which influenced much of the McKinsey research) what is needed is some modification or reinterpretation of the eight attributes to make them fit the UK local government environment.

Eight characteristics of organisational excellence

As set out in ISOE – that is, before any modification – the eight characteristics of the excellent company which Peters and Waterman saw in 1982 as essential to business success were as follows:

- **A bias for action:** getting on with things, experimenting and implementing; rather than paralysis by analysis. 'Don't just stand there: do something!'
- **Close to the customer:** listening to the customer; an obsession with quality service.
- **Autonomy and entrepreneurship:** encouraging innovation; identifying and supporting 'champions'; not being afraid to make mistakes.
- **Productivity through people:** treating everyone throughout the whole workforce as the root source of quality and productivity gains; motivation through 'hoopla' and the celebration of success.
- **Hands-on, value-driven:** creating an exciting and productive environment through the promotion of shared values and the personal energy and example of top management.
- **Stick to the knitting:** concentrating on the business the company knows and does best; 'back to basics'.
- **Simple form, lean staff:** simple organisation structures, flat management hierarchies; small corporate headquarters.
- **Simultaneous loose-tight qualities:** extensive devolution and managerial autonomy within a firmly maintained set of key values or standards.

Criticisms of the rational model

Before considering how these ideas can be applied to a UK local authority, it is interesting to look at a chapter in ISOE which has received far less attention than the eight principles. This chapter criticised what the authors described as "the rational model... the numerative, rationalist approach to management which dominates the business schools". This is the approach which has been particularly common in the UK public sector, and which places a major emphasis on functions such as cost-benefit analysis, strategic planning and management by statistically defined objectives. The emphasis is also on efficiency and cost savings, rather than effectiveness. Many of the Audit Commission's recommendations in its numerous reports and discussion papers fall into this rational category. The underlying philosophy is that organisational action and managerial decision-making can best be determined by the application of strictly rational or logical criteria and that, in the words of one local authority chief executive who ought to have known better, "if you can't measure something it doesn't exist".

Peters and Waterman launched a heavy attack on this rationalist approach which probably has at least as much, if not more, relevance to the public as to the private sector. The comment in ISOE that for many American managers, analytical planning is more intellectually satisfying than doing, does not seem a thousand miles away from the attitudes of at least some UK local officers in corporate or strategic planning units. ISOE also suggested that a naive belief in the virtues of performance-related pay is another symptom of an over-reliance on a rationalist approach, and that too has echoes throughout the UK public sector. The book caricatures this as a simplistic assumption that "if we give people big, straightforward monetary incentives to be smart and work right, the productivity problem will go away".

Why does the wholly rational approach fail to deliver? Peters and Waterman suggest eight reasons, most of which can be applied with very little modification to UK local authorities.

- It leads to an obsession with cost, rather than quality and value, with cost reduction then becoming the number one priority. Managers tend to analyse and concentrate on what can most easily be measured and analysed in statistical terms – that is, expenditure. Important 'soft' values (like equality, openness, responsiveness) are overlooked or sidelined. Local authorities criticised for exhibiting this far from unknown type of attitude may defend themselves by arguing that financial constraints and the rigours of CCT dictate cost-centred priorities. However, other more imaginative councils are well able to demonstrate that so-called soft values can be maintained and are worth maintaining, even in an environment which requires rigorous cost control.

- It also leads to "an abstract, heartless philosophy". It values institutions, structures and systems more than people and "takes the living element out of situations that should, above all, be alive". A micro example would be the authority which pursued an elderly man dying of cancer through the courts for payment of a very small sum of arrears of poll tax. The 'correct', rational process is for all arrears to be treated equally: but how much better to modify what may be legally right by the exercise of a little imagination and humanity – neither of these qualities being statistically measurable.

- The strictly rational approach tends to be negative. "It is inherently easier to develop a negative argument than to advance a constructive one". Or as Peter Drucker had pointed out earlier, if top managers perceive their role as saying 'yes' or 'no' to ideas as they come up, their tendency will be to veto new ideas as impractical. Many staff in local authorities suffer from just such an attitude on the part of their senior managers, and this stems in part from the difficulty the rational manager has in quantifying the benefits of ideas which, because they are not yet implemented, cannot be accurately costed.

- The strictly rational approach "does not value experimentation and abhors mistakes". This is largely an extension of the previous point. By definition, the rational, quantified approach is always searching for precision. It has also to treat any error as wholly negative because the costs of mistakes have to be entered on the non-productive side of the accountants' books. But often only experimentation will show whether a new idea will work and in any experiment there must always be the possibility of failure. In the rational organisation, the question asked when a mistake is made is: 'who was at fault?' In the more effective organisation, the question is: 'what can we learn?'.

- The cautious approach engendered by rationality leads to over-complex structures and systems. To safeguard against possible mistakes, an increasing number of checks and balances are built into the structure by adding supervisory levels to the hierarchy or by establishing specialist planning, analytical and monitoring units. To provide ever more data for analytical and control purposes, administrative and information systems become ever more complicated. While many local authorities have recognised these tendencies in recent years and reacted by, for example, simplifying their organisational structures, continual vigilance is necessary to prevent unnecessary complexity creeping back in. The very common 'solution' in many authorities to any new problem or requirement has been to create a specialist post to deal with it – usually argued on an apparently rational basis which committees find it difficult, logically, to resist.

- The rationalist approach promotes formality of system and management style and so fails to obtain the benefits of informality. Rational managers feel most comfortable when everything is defined and measurable. The verbs of the rational process are analyse, plan, specify, instruct, check – and these can be built into formal procedures and job roles. Yet in today's uncertain and changing environment, verbs such as interact, try, learn, adapt, modify are more appropriate – but are not susceptible to formal, rational prescription.

- The rational model denigrates the importance of values. Peters and Waterman comment that they observed few, if any, bold new company directions coming from rational analysis. While recognising that good companies have superb analytical skills, the authors of ISOE believed that crucial company decisions are shaped more by their values than by 'dexterity with numbers'. Excellent companies create 'a broad, uplifting, shared culture' which encourages their people to produce new ideas. The importance of values in a local authority context was discussed in chapter 2: here it need simply be noted that an over-emphasis on quantified rationality can inhibit the otherwise powerful influence of many of the qualitative values which are particularly relevant to public services.

- There is no place for internal competition in the rational model – the rational company does not compete with itself. This is the comment which has least relevance for local authorities. It is not referring to an internal purchaser/provider split but to direct commercial competition between different company divisions. Peters and Waterman found that many of the companies they described as excellent allowed or encouraged the existence of overlapping divisions and duplicated product development teams which competed with each other in the design of new products and in the fight for a share of company resources. The local authority parallel would be two council-run leisure centres on the same site which competed with each other for business, or two in-house and overlapping refuse collection services. While the idea of such head-on internal competition may have an appeal to some managers (and political market dogmatists), it would be difficult to justify the costs of duplication involved. Even in a private sector context, Peters and Waterman admit that while such costs are relatively easy to calculate, the revenue benefits stemming from internal competition are 'harder, if not impossible, to get a handle on'.

Some of the eight characteristics of excellent companies listed earlier may not seem so directly applicable to local authorities as these criticisms of the rational model. They are, however, well worth serious consideration and can provide an additional, though complementary checklist to 7-S.

The eight success factors and local authorities

A bias for action: Local authorities cannot generally take quite so buccaneering an approach to action as Peters and Waterman applaud in the entrepreneurial company. Their quote (from a Cadbury director) of "Ready. Fire. Aim!" may be acceptable when a company decides to risk its own money with a new product launch, but local authorities must be responsible in their use of public funds and are often dealing with issues which require extensive consultation and careful preparation. There is a case, however, for suggesting that councils (and individual managers) are sometimes too cautious or dilatory about getting things done. At council level, awkward decisions may be deferred by continual requests by elected members for further reports or by setting up reviews which may do little to clarify the issues and merely act as a delaying mechanism. Fine words in policy or mission statements are not always backed by practical and effective supporting action. At the managerial level, discussions about strategy and objectives do not always conclude with clear decisions about who is to do what and by when. The use of deadlines is particularly weak in some authorities. Agreement is reached about a course of action but without setting start and finish dates. Deadlines, even when set, tend to be treated as little more than the desirable but not essential dates for action to be completed, rather than as the latest acceptable date for completion and something to be bettered if at all possible.

Of course, many councils and managers are fully aware of the advantages of moving swiftly on issues which do not require lengthy analysis or discussion, but others could improve their effectiveness and reputation by adopting 'a bias for action'. This is partly a matter of systems and structures. Complex management hierarchies often involve processes which unnecessarily require even relatively simple proposals for action to be referred up the line for comment and approval. Systems which require all committee reports to be vetted and endorsed by central functions such as the finance, legal and equality units may cause lengthy delays in proposals reaching committees. Elected members who delight in requisitioning decisions of panels and committees for submission to full council may also set back action for many weeks. But a bias towards inaction is also a matter of attitudes. A fear of being proved wrong, a search for analytical precision, and reluctance to stop talking and start doing, are all symptoms of the delaying disease. Authorities with an excellent public reputation are generally those which pleasantly surprise their citizens and communities with the speed with which they address local issues of concern.

Close to the customer: This is probably the one factor on which all authorities would agree with the importance given to it by Peters and Waterman. The evolutionary implementation of customer-care policies and practices has been a remarkably extensive development in local government during the past decade. Anecdotal evidence suggests that in at least some cases this has been influenced by managers reading ISOE or attending Tom Peters' seminars at which he has continually hammered home the theme of high quality customer service. This theme has also been promoted strongly by the Local Government Management Board, the Audit Commission and the Citizens' Charter Initiative and does not therefore need to be argued for here as any kind of new idea or initiative.

It is worth noting, however, that ISOE – together with many other commentators – saw customer responsiveness as going well beyond the obvious principles of courtesy, speed of response, and good complaints procedures. They saw these as only half the story. The other half, they argued, was to see customers as a vital source of information and ideas. As they put it: "The excellent companies are not only better on service, quality, reliability... They are also better listeners... The fact that these companies are so strong on quality, service and the rest comes in large measure from... listening. From inviting the customer into the company. The customer is truly in partnership with the effective company...". In a local government context, this implies treating citizens as more than mere consumers. It points to initiatives of a kind which a growing number of councils are at least experimenting with, such as setting up user focus groups to discuss service developments, offering membership of consultative panels to local interest groups, providing public question sessions at council meetings, and forming committees of tenants, leisure centre users and the like. Despite the growth of the customer concept, there is very considerable scope for a variety of imaginative new measures to involve citizens, service users and interest groups more closely in the development and monitoring of council services.

Perhaps, too, it is desirable to use the term 'customer' a little less, and 'citizen' and 'community' more. The relationship between a council and its local population is far richer and more complex than the private sector relationship of company and customer. The Northtown Borough Council should be the servant and voice of the Northtown community – a very different relationship from that of the purchaser of a bar of fruit and nut with Cadburys.

Autonomy and entrepreneurship: This characteristic, as described in ISOE, needs to be treated with a good deal of caution and considerable modification before it can be applied to local authorities. The emphasis given by Peters and Waterman to what they described as 'fired up champions' and to a readiness to innovate and accept mistakes is wholly understandable in a fiercely competitive private sector market. They argue that some business initiatives are bound to fail, so the only way to guarantee securing some successes is to maximise the number of initiatives – as they put it: "The probability of something succeeding is very high if you try lots of things". In his usual flamboyant manner, Tom Peters develops this theme in his seminars by telling managers they are failures unless they make big mistakes.

The concept of encouraging and backing champions – pioneers of change who are prepared to challenge convention – is certainly one which all organisations, public and private sector, should take on board. Too often, conformity to the established way of doing things stifles innovation. But local authorities cannot be so cavalier about making mistakes as Peters and Waterman recommend. Significant risk-taking where public health and safety are concerned is not an acceptable option. Major errors in handling planning matters or in processes such as taking children into care have major adverse consequences. A local authority's assets are not private property for members or managers to gamble with on risky entrepreneurial ventures. The challenge is to combine the encouragement of innovation with a deep sense of responsibility for using public resources wisely – and that is far more difficult than the free-ranging approach which ISOE suggests is appropriate for the private sector.

Productivity through people: If only one factor had to selected from the Peters and Waterman list as universally applicable to organisations of all types and sizes, this is it. 'People are our most important asset' has become the management cliche of the 1990s – and that, perhaps, is the problem. Everyone agrees that the skill and commitment of its workforce is a primary source of high performance and success, and it is unnecessary to read all the detail and examples in ISOE to make the point. Most managers will say there is no need for a lengthy case to be made for this view – it is self evident. There can be few, if any, local authorities which would take a contrary view, and the growing number of councils which have achieved an Investors in People award is evidence that the rhetoric is being translated by these authorities into at least partial reality. (Partial, because IIP does not address every aspect of people management). But there are still many employers, including local authorities, who endorse the concept of productivity and quality through people, without any real change in managerial attitudes and with little idea of the range of action needed to give the concept practical effect. In addition, another buzzword of the 1990s – 'flexibility' – is often being interpreted in ways which have a directly damaging effect on employees' morale and commitment.

Peters and Waterman rightly argued that the basic requirements for maximising the contribution employees can make to a business are 'respect for the individual' and 'treating people as adults'. Employees' perceptions of these factors are influenced as much by the characteristics of managers' everyday informal relationships with their people as by formal personnel procedures or schemes. They are matters of managerial attitude, without which it is unlikely that any organisation will commit itself to the practical policies and measures which these beliefs imply. What are these measures? The examples quoted in ISOE suggest that the following eight issues are involved, and Peters and Waterman emphasise the need for a comprehensive approach which embraces all of these:

- Providing the highest possible level of job security.
- Extensive, continuous and honest communication.
- Giving a high priority to training and development.
- Enthusiastic encouragement of employees to contribute their ideas for improving productivity, service and quality.
- Employee involvement in decision-making.
- Setting high standards and achieving them through mutually high expectations and peer review.
- Generating excitement and a sense of achievement by celebrating success ('hoopla').
- Informality and an absence or minimisation of status distinctions.

Many of these issues are considered in more detail in chapter 6. Here, two points are worth some emphasis. Firstly, the rapid growth in the use of temporary and fixed term contracts by many authorities in the name of flexibility is undermining job security – one of the key factors, according to ISOE. Secondly, as the case studies conducted for the Audit Commission's 1995 People, Pay and Performance study showed, there are many examples of excellent practice by individual authorities in one or two of these personnel approaches, but very few in which a comprehensive and coordinated approach has been adopted which includes all eight.

Hands on – value-driven: The importance of shared values was discussed in some detail in chapter 2 and is not therefore developed here. It may be noted, however, that ISOE goes as far as suggesting that the definition and promotion of values (or basic beliefs) may well be the most important single success factor. Peters and Waterman say: "We doubt whether it is possible to be an excellent company without clarity on values and without having the right sort of values".

The 'hands on' part of this factor refers to the importance of top managers as role models in the promotion of an organisation's values. If values such as openness, respect for individuals and responsiveness to customers have been publicised, the chief executive and chief officers had better behave in ways which demonstrate their personal commitment to these ideals. Being restrictive or selective with information, standing on dignity and being reluctant to admit mistakes will soon be recognised by staff at large – and the public – as evidence that the value statements are no more than publicity puffs. There is a further point: it is difficult for top managers to act as role models unless they are visible and are seen to have a keen interest in work at the front-line. Peters and Waterman noted that the chief executives of successful companies were almost all proponents of MBWA – management by wandering around. They spent little time in their own offices. They got out and about, meeting with and discussing issues with staff at all levels, and visiting customers and suppliers to find out about plans and problems and help cultivate effective partnerships.

There is a lesson here for local authorities. The current trend for a separation of strategic and operational functions, with the chief executive and just two or three directors forming the strategic team, would seem to carry a significant risk of top managerial invisibility so far as the majority of staff are concerned. Attention to strategy needs to be paralleled by a demonstrable understanding of the realities of operational work. Anecdotal evidence about UK local authorities confirms ISOE's findings that the most effective chief executives are those who are hands-on in the sense of maintaining close personal touch with front-line staff, and who are more likely to be found out in the community than behind their desks in the town hall.

Stick to the knitting: If this principle applies at all to local authorities – and this is a matter of debate – it needs to be thought through very carefully. It is superficially attractive because of the simplicity and comfort of the message. Just concentrate on what you do best. But what is a local authority's knitting? What do, or should, authorities do best?

Peters and Waterman's main theme under this heading was to question the commercial viability of conglomerates. They did not oppose some diversification of a company's activities, but claimed that the most successful firms 'diversified around a single skill'. Conversely, they argued that the least successful companies were those which diversified into a wide variety of fields, with no unifying skill or know-how factor. On this analysis, if local authorities were viewed as businesses, most would fail. Local authorities are inherently multi-functional organisations, involved in a wide variety of activities which have few common specialist skills. Finding a common skills base (apart from general management expertise) between, say, leisure services, environmental health and strategic planning is all but impossible. Moreover, local authorities do not have the freedom of commercial companies to decide what businesses they are in. A council cannot opt out of the planning function simply because it is not particularly good at it.

The knitting principle has been quoted by some commentators and politicians as a justification for extensive outsourcing by councils of support functions. The argument is that local authorities are good at providing mainstream services but have no particular skills in cleaning, catering, payroll management, training and the like. This argument is very suspect. Once it is accepted that councils have to be conglomerates – in the sense of having to be involved in a wide range of disparate activities – there is no technical reason why an authority should not develop as much expertise in, say, office cleaning or debt collection as it does in refuse collection or processing planning applications.

It may be helpful, however, to define what local authorities should be good at – their real knitting. In broad terms, this amounts to two things:

- The effective management of the provision of a wide range of public services.
- The provision of a democratically produced voice for the local community and a focus for the identification and promotion of measures to meet local needs.

Sticking to these principles will avoid arid arguments about the pros and cons of outsourcing and any over-concentration on the development or disbandment of one function, simply because at the moment the authority has or has not the necessary expertise. It will focus attention on authorities' vital role as a lobbyist for the community and as a catalyst and co-ordinator for action, whether or not this is handled directly. And it will avoid the trap which some of ISOE's 'excellent' companies later fell into of concentrating so fully on what they happened to do well in 1980 that they failed to change course to adapt to the new world of the 1990s.

Simple form, lean staff: In considering ISOE's arguments about this principle, it must be remembered that the book was commenting on very large companies, most operating across the whole of the USA and many internationally. For example, Johnson & Johnson was quoted as a $5 billion business with 150 independent divisions, and 3M was commended for its policy of establishing a new independent division whenever a part of the company topped $20 million in annual turnover. Updated to the late 1990s and applied to local government, this 3M principle would imply that all district authorities are well below the size which ISOE considered suitable for a single unified management. Chopping a district, or even a London borough, into dozens of often quasi-autonomous business units does not necessarily accord with Peters and Waterman's interpretation of simplicity of form or the beauty of smallness. Small is relative – and the relative in ISOE is huge.

Peters and Waterman suggest an approach to organisational structure consisting of what they describe as three pillars:

- The 'stability pillar' provides a basic, simple, underlying structural principle – which ISOE suggest should be product-based divisions for manufacturing companies.
- The 'entrepreneurial pillar' is based on the principle of small is beautiful – constantly hiving off new or expanded activities into new divisions to facilitate responsiveness to the market.
- The 'habit-breaking pillar' involves a readiness to reorganise regularly to adapt to new threats or opportunities.

There are some ideas here of relevance to local authorities but others which should not be accepted without question. Many social services departments, for example, find it advantageous to structure themselves on the basis of client groups – children, the elderly, the mentally handicapped and so on. Organising to optimise the convenience of service users is a related principle of very wide application. The small is beautiful approach needs more caution. ISOE admits that it can result in inefficiencies, and local authorities need to balance any advantages of small, self-contained units against what, for some functions at least, are the economies of scale. In many authorities there would be no need to argue for a willingness to reorganise regularly – the complaint is that reorganisations have been far too frequent. There is a balance to be struck between ossification and continual frenetic change, and this is a matter for local judgement and good sense. The answers will not be found in a book.

The other element of this principle is 'lean staff', by which Peters and Waterman meant the size of the corporate headquarters – not head-cutting in the workforce at large. They quote companies with 50,000 or so staff with only 100 in their corporate headquarters. For local authorities, the size of HQ or central staffing is largely determined by the extent to which functions such as finance and personnel have been, or can be, decentralised – and this, in turn, is largely a matter of size. The three-person personnel unit in a small district council cannot be chopped into eight pieces and devolved to eight service departments. The 80 strong centralised personnel and training unit in a county or large unitary can devolve at least two-thirds of its staff to operational service departments.

If the possibly centralising impact of CCT is ignored, the inclusion of financial, personnel and IT specialists within the management teams of at least the major departments has generally proved far more effective than the retention of large, central support functions, operating through the bureaucracy of service level agreements (SLAs). To quote a CIPFA view:

> "The decentralisation of functions in many authorities is moreover having the effect of breaking up support services... into small units dedicated to DSOs and single services... SLAs may not then be necessary or even practicable... There is usually only one user for the services which their staff provide so there is seldom any point in drawing up SLAs for them. Their cost is often satisfactorily treated as a direct cost".[1]

The effect of decentralisation on the relative size of central functions can be illustrated by statistics from the Audit Commission's *Quality Exchange* for personnel services.[2] This quoted the numbers of central personnel staff per 1,000 employees as averaging 0.79 in counties and 5.57 in districts – though these figures were also influenced by apparent economies of scale in the large authorities. Total personnel staff (i.e. including clerical and administrative support, and inclusive of central and devolved staff) were shown in these statistics as 5.69 per 1,000 employees for counties and 14.89 for districts. Lean central staffing combined with economies in the volume of support services would seem to be significantly easier to achieve in large authorities.

Simultaneous loose-tight properties: The concept behind this rather clumsy phrase has a very direct relevance to local authorities. The idea is simple – extensive devolution of authority throughout the organisation within a framework of clearly articulated values or standards – or to use a simpler phrase than ISOEs, 'freedom within boundaries'.

This can be illustrated by one authority's approach to devolving a wide range of decision-making in the field of people management to unit managers. These managers now had the authority to make decisions about recruitment, promotion, training and rewards, giving them for the first time extensive control of their primary resource – their staff. The authority's message to these managers was, in effect: 'you now have the authority to manage your own staff – provided you do so to acceptable standards'. The proviso was important. The authority recognised its corporate responsibilities as an employer and the need to demonstrate commitment to values such as openness and equality in the way its staff were managed. Unit managers needed to be set free to make their own detailed staffing decisions, but not to the point at which one might adopt a macho fire and hire approach and another ignore the need for effective staff communication. The answer was to define a set of principles or standards of people management (not a conventional personnel procedure manual) to which all managers were required to conform. Within these boundaries, managers were free to manage.[3]

The same approach can be applied to a wide range of functions and managerial activities. In customer care, for example, each service can be free to design and operate its own monitoring and complaints procedures, provided these comply with one or two corporately defined principles – such as the principle that there must be a process for dealing with complaints from the public promptly and honestly. Managers with devolved decision-making authority may also need guidance to ensure they comply with the law, which in many instances sets the boundaries of freedom. Within the authority, the underlying but all pervasive set of guiding principles should, of course, be the authority's values, a point to which ISOE continually returns.

Was 'In Search of Excellence' wrong?

There has been a reaction against ISOE, caused largely by the fact that many of the companies selected by Peters and Waterman as excellent have since failed. Tom Peters himself, who separated from Waterman soon after ISOE was published, had the nerve to start his 1987 book, *Thriving on Chaos*, with the provocative statement: "There are no excellent companies". Waterman, however, has continued to support the principles set out in ISOE, and a closer look at the reasons for a number of the companies' failures points to two factors for which ISOE need not be blamed – with the possible exception of 'stick to the knitting':

- The characteristics of excellence in ISOE work well provided a company adopts the right business strategy. A classic example of getting this wrong is IBM, which for too long seemed to interpret its knitting as the production and leasing of mainframe computers, and as a consequence achieved a world record for the size of its losses and nearly collapsed.
- A related factor is complacency when things are going well and a consequent failure to change sufficiently quickly to respond to external change. This is Pascale's paradox of success breeding failure.

If the book was to be re-written today, it seems likely that one more factor would be added, rather than all the success factors being set aside. This new factor is one which both Peters and Waterman have since and separately addressed. For Peters, it is the ability to cope with constant and unpredictable change; Waterman has described it as the renewal factor, emphasising qualities such as opportunism, habit-breaking and the ability to view the organisation from an external perspective. In other words, skill in managing change, or in one word, adaptability. It is a factor which underlies many of the ideas considered in the remaining chapters of this book.

Footnotes:
1. CIPFA: *The Management of Overheads in Local Authorities*, 1991.
2. Audit Commission: *The Quality Exchange: Personnel Services*, 1991.
3. Berkshire County Council: *Specification for Devolved Human Resource Management*, 1992.

Chapter 4

Business process re-engineering

Only experience over the next decade will prove whether business process re-engineering (BPR) is a passing fashion of the 1990s or a concept which will have an enduring impact on how organisations operate. The topic – which has nothing to do with engineering in the industrial sense – has generated fierce debate among academics, consultants and managers, here and in the USA. Some argue that it is downright damaging – 'a fad that forgets people' as Tom Davenport, one of the original proponents of BPR, described it after changing his mind about the concept. Others, including Michael Hammer and James Champy (the 1993 authors of *Re-engineering the Corporation*, the principal book on the subject)[1] claim that BPR is the only approach which will secure business success in a world of global competition. Whatever the pros and cons, the fact is that many companies have embarked on re-engineering initiatives, while in the public sector the principles of BPR are influencing organisational change in a number of Civil Service agencies and in NHS trusts. Some local authority members and managers have also become attracted to the concept and are applying it to the redesign of functions and organisation structures.

The fact that BPR is the subject of widely differing views indicates that it is worth examining in some detail – strong ideas generate strong responses. But common sense and a study of the history of earlier messages from the management gurus suggest that the truth about its relevance and value lies somewhere between the two extremes of opinion which enliven the current debate. Because of its emphasis on commercial success for large American corporations in the global private sector marketplace, its applicability to UK local government needs also to be considered with care.

The background to BPR

Michael Hammer, originally a mathematician and later the most outspoken BPR enthusiast, has claimed that re-engineering represents a fundamentally new approach. 'Reversing the Industrial Revolution' is how he has modestly put it, arguing that re-engineering re-assembles tasks and functions which the 19th century principles of the division of labour took apart. But hyperbole of this kind is unhelpful because it fails to recognise that many elements in BPR have antecedents going back some 50 years.

Some of BPR's basic principles are remarkably similar to aspects of two techniques with which all local authorities are familiar – work study and O&M (organisation and methods). Both these techniques involve the systematic study of working procedures and claim that by a process of analysis and redesign it is possible to evolve 'the one best way' of doing anything. Work study deals principally with physical or manual work, O&M with administrative and non-manual processes. In both cases, one of the basic principles is that the aim should be not simply to identify improvements to the way things are currently being done, but to question whether current activities need to be done at all. Work study has become discredited largely because of the failure of the manual worker bonus schemes with which the technique became identified in the late 1960s. As a result, the potential benefits of the baby of method study have been thrown out with the dirty bathwater of bad bonusing. O&M has been increasingly side-lined by developments in computerisation. Many O&M specialists failed to jump onto the IT bandwagon and as a result, much of their work in the study and redesign of office procedures has been taken over by systems analysts. As with work study and O&M, systems analysts have always been urged to ask fundamental questions about the processes subject to potential computerisation – not just to produce computerised versions of existing manual systems. IT offers opportunities to completely re-think the need for, and nature of, many tasks and procedures – very much in line with BPR principles.

Another approach with BPR connections is value analysis (VA), sometimes termed value management or value engineering. VA in an industrial context was developed by Lawrence Miles in the USA in the late 1940s, and later adopted by the US Navy and the Pentagon as a method of assessing major capital projects. It is used extensively in Japan and has recently been promoted in the UK by the Department of Trade and Industry. VA is discussed in more detail in chapter 10 because of its link with quality, but is mentioned here because it involves the fundamental reassessment of processes within an organisation, and brainstorming to produce possibly wholly new ways of working – all consistent with BPR principles.

BPR principles

Hammer and Champy have defined BPR as:

"The fundamental rethinking and radical redesign of business processes to achieve dramatic improvements in critical contemporary measures of performance such as cost, quality, service and speed".

They say the key words in this definition are 'fundamental', 'processes' and 'dramatic', emphasising the idea that to be effective, the redesign of a process should start with a clean sheet of paper and not attempt simply to improve what is currently being done. Michael Hammer would not agree with the commonly held notion that you have to start from where you are at.

It is not possible to grasp the BPR concept without first understanding the meaning placed on the word 'process'. Hammer defines a process as "a set of business activities that create a value" – a definition which needs some interpretation if it is to be applied to the functions of a local authority. In BPR terms, a process is not a single procedure or task. It is a collection or sequence of all the tasks which taken together produce an end result. One example in the personnel field might be the whole process of filling a vacant post, which involves a series of procedures or activities – from the initial production of a job description and person specification, through advertising and selection, to the offer and acceptance of an appointment and the new employee actually starting work. Subjecting this process to a BPR scrutiny would involve setting aside all the current procedures and considering, from scratch, what needs to be done to achieve the quickest and most cost-effective way of moving from the occurrence of a vacancy to its being filled. The result might, in Hammer and Champy's terms, be a fundamental and dramatic new approach. Other examples of processes might be the handling of a planning application from its initial receipt to its resolution, or the administration of a council election from its first announcement to the registration of new members at their first council meeting.

A problem some managers have with BPR is that although Hammer and Champy go into considerable detail about the symptoms of what they describe as process dysfunction and about the characteristics of re-engineered processes done well or badly, their book is extremely thin on what the process of re-engineering itself should consist of. In other words, they describe why re-engineering is necessary and what happens after it has been done, but say little about how to do it. However, in a section of their book about 'making it happen' they suggest five roles are needed for a successful re-engineering campaign:

- A leader, who authorises the campaign and motivates those involved.
- 'Process owners', managers with responsibility for each process under review.
- Re-engineering teams, to carry out the diagnosis and redesign of each process.
- A steering committee, to exercise policy oversight across all the teams.
- A 're-engineering czar', to develop the necessary re-engineering techniques and tools throughout the organisation, although the book does not explain what these tools and techniques are.

The implication is that once a process has been identified, re-engineering starts with a diagnosis of its purpose and the identification of symptoms which may indicate flaws in how it is currently being carried out. To emphasise the value of completely fresh thinking – the starting from scratch approach – Hammer and Champy say it is not necessary for a re-engineering team to know much about the current process. The whole emphasis is on a fundamental redesign, not on tweaking current tasks and procedures. The main symptom of 'process dysfunction' (i.e. badly designed processes) is what they describe as the 'fragmentation of a natural process', evidenced by:

- Excessive exchange of information between various parts of the process.
- A high ratio of checking and control to activities which add value.
- Time delays between the various stages in the process.
- Time spent correcting errors.
- A large volume of special cases – circumstances which the routine process cannot deal with.

Hammer and Champy go into more detail about the common features of processes which have been successfully redesigned, and these provide further clues about the factors which a re-engineering team should consider. The book, which tends to be somewhat repetitive, lists nearly 20 features, but these can be summarised as follows:

- Tasks currently undertaken separately in relatively simple jobs are combined to form skilled, multi-functional jobs.
- The stages in a process are performed in their natural order.
- Processes may have multiple versions to cope with varying circumstances.
- Work is performed where it is best done – which may imply outsourcing some parts of the process.
- There is a reduction in the volume of checking and control.
- Rewards are given for the achievement of results, not simply for activity.
- Work units (i.e. sections or departments) change from being organised on functional lines to become process teams.
- Managerial hierarchies are reduced and organisation structures are flattened.
- Customers have a single point of contact.
- There is total compatibility between processes, the nature of jobs and structures, management methods, and the organisation's values and beliefs.
- IT is recognised and exploited as offering many opportunities for the redesign of work systems and the provision of information to enhance devolved decision making.

Linked to these generally 'hard' characteristics of the way work, jobs and organisation are re-designed, Hammer and Champy list several 'soft' factors which many organisations' BPR enthusiasts seem to have overlooked. They refer to the need for management changing from control to empowerment, for a shift from narrowly focused staff training to broader education, for a change of values, and for managers to become leaders rather than 'scorekeepers'. They even talk of workers making decisions. Unfortunately, the emphasis of many re-engineering initiatives in industry has been on stripping out levels of management, downsizing (sacking large numbers of staff) and cost-cutting, with little apparent regard for the effect on employee morale and motivation.

Hammer and Champy's own analysis of common errors in re-engineering includes the neglect of values and beliefs and an over-concentration on the technicalities of the redesign process, along with:

- A willingness to settle for only minor improvements.
- Placing prior constraints on the outcome and thus inhibiting innovative thinking.
- Skimping on the resources needed by the re-engineering teams.
- Allowing the existing corporate culture to prevent the acceptance of new ways of doing things.
- Having a leader who does not understand the BPR philosophy.
- Quitting too early.

They also say that 're-engineering never happens from the bottom' and must always be driven top-down – a view a little difficult to reconcile with their endorsement of empowerment to staff in the front-line.

BPR in practice

Studies by academics and consultants of actual BPR projects quote failure rates as high as 75%, and Hammer himself has expressed concern about the way many companies have equated BPR with 'slash and burn' cost cutting. "Re-engineering", he now says, "is about rethinking work, not eliminating jobs", though the title of an early article of his in the Harvard Business Review – *Re-engineering Work: Don't Automate; Obliterate* – did not exactly discourage the idea of the wholesale disbandment of jobs. Moreover, in a curious parallel to *In Search of Excellence*, companies which Hammer and Champy claimed in their book to have mounted effective BPR campaigns have since been shown by Tom Davenport to have fared badly in commercial terms. Davenport, whose book, *Process Innovation* preceded Hammer and Champy's better known work, now says: "The rock that re-engineering foundered on is simple: people". Too often, he suggests, BPR exercises have failed to take account of human factors, treating employees as "just so many bits and bytes: interchangeable parts to be re-engineered".

In a UK magazine article in 1996 entitled *Business Process Re-engineering RIP*,[2] Edith Mumford (a Manchester University professor) and Rick Hendricks (an American consultant) saw the neglect of human variables as a major cause of BPR failures, but also pointed to several other reasons:

- Too many organisations, they said, launched BPR projects simply to copy others, without thinking through what they were doing or trying to achieve.
- There was no theory to guide organisations in the BPR process. Macho managers were attracted by the message: 'Do it fast, fiercely and without much thought'. This approach might be necessary for a company verging on bankruptcy but was not a sensible strategy for an organisation which was doing quite well and simply wanted to do better.
- Too many organisations were allowing consultants to drive the BPR process. Managers were too busy to spend the necessary time on a detailed diagnosis of their organisations' processes, so consultants were hired. Unfortunately, say Mumford and Hendricks, because Hammer and Champy had not spelt out a BPR methodology, consultants were able to use their old analytical

techniques and claim they were re-engineering. Computer vendors joined in to sell the new hardware and software which the consultants often recommended, and managements then needed to make cuts to justify the costs of the whole exercise.

Less cynically, Mumford and Hendricks emphasised that if an organisation wishes to achieve the radical type of transformation which BPR implies, it may well require a major change of culture. The concept of organisational culture is dealt with in more detail in chapter 7. It is enough here to point out that if the style of a redesigned process differs significantly from the overall character or style of the organisation as a whole, it is unlikely it can be implemented successfully. A fast, responsive, loosely monitored process will not 'take' in an organisation which is characterised by qualities of caution, precision and close central control.

There is, however, another side to the BPR coin. This is the enthusiasm for re-engineering by organisations which have applied the concept successfully. In 1995, the Institute of Personnel and Development (IPD) published a paper[3] which described five such success stories in the UK. Four were in the private sector – Toshiba at Plymouth, Bass, Rank Xerox and the Royal Bank of Scotland. All reported major improvements in business performance as a result of sweeping re-engineered change. All said that part of this success was due to their taking full account of cultural and people issues within the re-BPR process. In the public sector, the BPR star was the Leicester Royal Infirmary. As one example of over 100 re-engineered processes, the hospital quoted a reduction from 79 hours to 34 minutes of the time between a doctor making a request for a test and receiving the result, while the waiting time for operations has been cut by almost 50%. Mike Oram, vice-president of the IPD, ascribed the hospital's achievements to "the audacious pursuit of what was previously unthinkable", while a consultant neurologist saw the key to success as dealing with all the pieces of each process, rather than examining processes piecemeal. The focus in this Leicester hospital has been on improving the quality of patient care, not on cost-cutting, and there have been only 42 redundancies among the trust's 4,500 employees. Staff and unions seem enthusiastic about the whole exercise, which has included a significant emphasis on the design of more satisfying jobs and on training to raise the level and range of employees' skills.

The four main lessons to be learned from organisations which have applied the BPR concept successfully appear to be:

- Be clear about the organisation's core values and ensure that proposed new ways of working are consistent with these values and the overall culture.
- Within this broad influence of values and culture, think fundamentally about new and better ways of working, always keeping the end purpose of every process in mind. Do not be inhibited by precedent. Exploit IT in the design of new work systems.
- Consider the linkages between various tasks and functions and look at processes as a whole – do not redesign things on a piecemeal basis.

- Involve people in the whole process and bear in mind at all times that the ultimate success of any fundamental change depends on the willingness and ability of people to implement it.

BPR for local authorities

The emphasis in BPR on processes, as distinct from individual tasks or procedures, is of direct relevance to many local government activities. Traditionally, local authorities' organisation structures have been based on the separate identity of the various professions – legal, financial, engineering and the like. Because many activities require the involvement of more than one profession or functional group, processes – in the BPR sense of the word – have involved various stages and procedures in which a case or decision is passed from one unit to another before a final outcome is achieved. Processes, in other words, are fragmented. This fragmentation is exacerbated by traditional management hierarchies. In addition to an issue passing between units, it may also be passed up and down the hierarchy within each unit, with junior staff drafting letters or reports which have to be vetted by their seniors before despatch, or authority having to be obtained from some central point before any action can be taken.

Two risks occur every time an issue is referred from one person or unit to another:

- Poor communication between different parts of the whole process may lead to misunderstanding or distortion of the subject matter; or something vital may be missed because there was a lack of clarity about the role and responsibility of each participant. As Hammer says, "Every time there's a hand-off there's a major opportunity for error".
- Time delays occur between each part of the process, as each person concerned puts their part of the process into an actual or metaphorical pending tray while clearing other parts of their jobs.

The risk of lengthy delays and of important aspects falling through the gaps in a process can be seen most dramatically in the reports of enquiries into failures in childcare. The BPR process in these cases is the sequence of activities involved from the first indication that a child may need protection to protective action being taken. In almost every report on cases of child abuse, poor communication and misunderstandings between the various agencies involved are quoted as major causes of failure, linked to delays and confusion about who was responsible for what within each agency. Following the publication of enquiry reports, spokespersons for the local authorities involved almost always announce that "we have revised our procedures in the light of the report's conclusions" – or words to that effect. What may really be needed is a not just an adjustment to existing procedures but a fundamental review of the whole process. Of course, in this example the practicability of carrying out a BPR review of the process is complicated by several agencies being involved – social services, the police, the health authority and perhaps a voluntary agency. None can dictate to the others. But it is the very complexity of the organisational situation which emphasises the need for a holistic view to be taken of the process and for clarity of responsibility and involvement to be achieved. A BPR team in these circumstances would need to draw membership from all the agencies involved. It should also concentrate on the integration of functions based on priority childcare objectives, not on the protection of separate professional identities. BPR exponents would recommend the inclusion in such a team of people who knew very little about the current ways of working, in order to ensure genuinely fresh thinking.

The related factor which applies to many local authority processes is the time delay between various activities in the whole process sequence. A very simple example might be an average time of two weeks between receipt of a request from a member of the public for a resident's parking permit and the issue of the permit. If the current process is examined, it is likely to show that the total, actual working time involved is less than one hour. An envelope is opened, the enclosed application form is checked, if it is satisfactory the brief details of the permit are keyed in, the computer prints out the permit with an addressed envelope, the permit is inserted in the envelope, the envelope is put with the outgoing post – perhaps 25 minutes of work activity. So why the two weeks turn-round time? It will probably be found that one person in the highway services department logs the receipt of the application form along with other of the department's post and then puts it in a tray for a porter to take to the car park section. The next day, the car park section clerk sorts the section's post and passes the form to whoever looks after residents' permits. It stays in that person's in-tray for two or three days while other work is being dealt with. It is then checked against the electoral register to ensure the applicant is a resident. That confirmed, the applicant's cheque is sent to the finance department where it is banked a day later and cleared four days after that. Nothing is done during this period. With the cheque cleared, the application is registered and passed to another person for the actual permit to be produced. At this point a further delay occurs. When the permit and its envelope have been printed, these are passed to the clerk in the department who deals with incoming and outgoing post. Four or five people in two departments and several sections will have been involved, with time delays occurring at every stage.

Similar major differences between working time and elapsed time are common in many local authority processes. Two examples are the turn-round time for simple planning applications and the time to process an application for housing benefit. Authorities may be very self-congratulatory for achieving planning turn-rounds of, say, eight weeks – but a log of actual working time on many planning applications would show that only a few hours actual work was involved on each. Lengthy delays in processing housing benefit claims may also result largely from discontinuities in the processing sequence. Delays of these kinds are a common source of customer dissatisfaction, contributing to the stereotype of the slow and insensitive town hall bureaucrat. The redesign of processes specifically to accelerate processing time is well worth the effort, and it is evident from a number of accounts of successful BPR projects that this has been one of their achievements.

The Leicester hospital's reduction of the time taken for a doctor to receive a test result from about two weeks to just over half an hour is just one of many similar examples.

The time factor also illustrates another very relevant BPR principle – that processes should be designed from the customer's viewpoint rather than for internal administrative convenience. This is an aspect on which many authorities have taken action in recent years. An example – not then labelled re-engineering but wholly in line with BPR practice – was a county council which rethought the way it processed student grants. Organised on conventional professional lines, the existing process involved two departments. On receipt of a grant application, the education department checked the student's eligibility on educational criteria. If satisfactory, the application was then passed to the finance department for details of the student's and parents' income to be checked and the grant eventually to be paid. Delays occurred between the education department approving a grant in principle and the finance department checking the monetary details and issuing the cheque. Students with queries were sometimes shunted backwards and forwards between the two departments. There was a tendency for each department to blame the other when an application form went missing. Two sets of records were kept – one in each department – with the consequent time and cost of duplication of entries of students' details. Each department jealously guarded its own professional interests.

Following complaints from students and parents about delays and confusion, a small working party was set up to redesign the whole process. The members of the working party were not drawn from the two departments concerned and had no previous detailed knowledge of the grants system. The outcome was the establishment of a single grants section, with staff trained to deal with both the educational and financial aspects of the process, and a streamlined application procedure designed for the convenience of applicants. Most applications could then be fully resolved and payments made dealt with within a day or two of their receipt – compared with delays of three or four weeks within the previous process.

BPR and 7-S

This last example indicates that BPR is not a wholly new concept. To a significant extent, it is the terminology which is new, not the practice of applying fresh thinking to the design of work processes. The publicity about BPR may, however, encourage more authorities to take a bolder look at processes as a whole, rather than just making incremental improvements to current procedures.

It needs to be remembered, though, that major changes of the kind which may result from fundamental fresh thinking may fail at the implementation stage unless the full implications of change are addressed. Mumford and Hendricks made the point in their article that "the success of a proposed change depends on the willingness of employees to accept it with enthusiasm and to implement it with care". Omitting this human element is a recipe for failure, although this is not the only factor to consider. This is where the 7-S concept , described in chapter 2, comes in.

Using the 7-S as a checklist, it can be seen that to be successful, process changes of the type generated by BPR reviews need to:
- Be consistent with the authority's shared values and style.
- Be influenced by corporate and service strategies.
- Mesh well with other systems.
- Either fit the structure or include structural change.
- Involve and motivate the staff.
- Secure any necessary new skills.

Footnotes:
1. *Re-engineering the Corporation*, Michael Hammer & James Champy, Brealey, 1993.
2. *Business Process Re-engineering RIP*, E Mumford and R Hendricks, *People Management*, 2nd May 1996.
3. *Re-engineering's Missing Ingredient: the Human Factor*, Institute of Personnel & Development, 1995.

Chapter 5

Management by objectives and performance management

Management has always been about getting things done and good managers have always been concerned to get the right things done well. That, in essence, is performance management – organising work to produce the best possible results. From this simple viewpoint, performance management is not a system or a technique. It is the totality of every competent manager's day-to-day activity. The problem is that managers vary considerably in their personal effectiveness, so performance standards may not be universally high. Additionally, there is no guarantee that all the managers in an organisation will work towards the same set of organisational priorities if the methods they use are left entirely to their individual initiative. So for many decades, the search has been on for the one best method of management which, by systematising good practice and defining organisational goals, will enable all managers to reach the standards of the best.

1971: Management by Objectives (MBO)

For many years, management textbooks described various processes – work planning, costing, production control, budgeting – but failed to set these different managerial activities within the overall framework of a total management system. So when John Humble, a director of Urwick Orr (the first British management consultancy), produced his book *Management by Objectives* in 1971, many managers thought that at long last they had been given a blueprint of effective management.

As with so many management concepts, the principles of management by objectives had been set out far earlier than its popular take-off by the grand-daddy of all gurus, Peter Drucker. Back in the 1950s he had written that every manager needed to work towards clearly defined and measurable objectives, and that these objectives should be drawn from 'the goals of the business enterprise'. However, he did not suggest any particular methodology for converting these principles into practice. Most managers who read Drucker probably accepted the logic of his ideas and assumed they were already applying them without the need for any formal system. After all, the idea that managers should know what they doing and that this should benefit the organisation was hardly revolutionary. Whether for this or other reasons, Drucker's views about objectives were not taken up as an important new management concept, and the subject lay relatively dormant until the late 1960s.

The complacency which characterised many managements in the 1950s evaporated during the next decade as commercial competition became fiercer. Organisations became more aware of the need to improve their performance and began turning to the relatively new profession of management consultancy for ideas and assistance to raise management standards. What they were looking for were not statements of principle but hard-edged methods or systems, and this is where John Humble came in and hit the consultancy jackpot. What his book and its subsequent development by Urwick Orr did was to take Drucker's principles, expand them and provide a detailed methodology or process for putting them into practical effect.

Management by objectives became the managerial buzzword of the early 1970s, discussed and applied so extensively that it was soon referred to universally as MBO. (One test of a new management concept is how rapidly and extensively it acquires an acronym, and in its day, MBO became at least as widely used as the more recent TQM, let alone BPR or VA).

Humble did not rely entirely on Drucker's ideas, but based his MBO system on a new definition and on the concept of an interlinked cycle of planning, objective-setting and review. His somewhat inelegant definition of management by objectives was:

> "The attempt to clarify the goals of management objectivity so that responsibility for achieving the goals was reasonably distributed round the management team, and to check standards of performance against which management effectiveness can be measured".

Left at this uninspiring statement, his book would probably have sunk without trace, but he rescued the situation by suggesting an attractively logical and comprehensive cycle of organisational and individual activity which could be driven by a set of detailed and documented procedures. The cycle consisted of:

- Strategic planning at the corporate level, generating strategic objectives.
- Tactical planning to support the strategic plans, generating tactical objectives.
- Unit or section planning, setting out the objectives for each part of the organisation.
- The allocation of defined responsibilities and objectives to each manager to ensure achievement of the corporate and unit objectives.
- The systematic review of managers', unit and corporate performance against the predetermined objectives.
- Feedback of the results of these reviews into the strategic, tactical and unit planning process, thus closing the loop.

Although this activity cycle appears to place a major emphasis on corporate planning and objectives, the MBO system developed by Humble and marketed by Urwick Orr, focused on objectives at the level of the individual manager. What was offered was an off-the-shelf manual and set of forms, providing a standardised approach to the definition and setting of individual objectives. Each management job had to be divided into 'key results areas' – inevitably referred to as KRAs. Objectives had to be set for each KRA and each objective had to be assessed by some form of measurement. For both objectives and their assessment, a strong emphasis was placed on quantifiable measurement. Objectives and assessments were to be reviewed and revised at an annual meeting between each manager and his or her senior – the principal origin of the annual appraisal interview. The whole procedure was to be documented, using a standard set of forms.

This system was introduced with enthusiasm by many companies who saw it as at last providing an objective and structured way of defining what to do and how well to do it.

For Urwick Orr it provided a consultancy bonanza, as Urwick had copyrighted much of the MBO material and many companies sought outside assistance in implementing the system and training managers in its operation. For a while, it did seem to offer the solution to many organisations' problems, yet within 10 years (and often much less), most companies had quietly abandoned the detailed system which Humble and Urwick had developed. Why? The reasons are worth examining because they provide clues about the probability of success or failure of the re-emergence in the 1990s of many MBO principles in the guise of PMS – performance management systems – as promoted in local government by the Audit Commission and the Local Government Management Board.

Why MBO systems failed

Part of the reason for the disappearance of the 1970s MBO has already been mentioned – the emphasis in the proprietary Urwick Orr system on objectives for individual managers without creating a strong enough link with corporate and unit objectives, despite John Humble's planning and review cycle. But there are several other reasons, in particular:

- Some chief executives used the system as a way of managing managers, rather than a way of managing performance. Managers in these circumstances saw the system as oppressive and appraisals as something to be feared or manipulated.
- The system was inherently bureaucratic in its requirement for extensive documentation and strict adherence to a timetabled sequence of activities. Operating the system became an end in itself, rather than a means to an end. There was just too much paperwork.
- The system was usually introduced as a top management decision, administered by central personnel or management services departments. Many managers resented this central imposition and influence, and saw the system as being 'owned' by specialists and constituting an additional chore, rather than as a new and helpful way of managing.
- There tended to be an over-emphasis on quantifiable as distinct from qualitative objectives, which in practice meant the dominance of financial indices and cost-cutting. Some MBO enthusiasts were proud of the slogan: 'If some-

thing can't be measured, it doesn't exist' – an indication of good sense having flown out of the managerial window.

- The rigid adherence to a formal annual cycle could not cope with a fast-moving commercial environment. The system was not sufficiently responsive to market realities.
- The insistence on everything being pre-planned inhibited innovation – new ideas cannot, by definition, be specified in advance.
- The use of an off-the-shelf proprietary system meant that organisations failed to adapt the MBO approach to their own characteristics and culture.
- The highly structured and precise procedures of MBO were better suited to public sector bureaucracies than to the companies facing growing market competition. Few entrepreneurial managers – though many administrators – were naturally as systematic as the MBO system demanded. But in the early 1970s, consultants did not generally see public sector organisations as potential clients, nor did many local authorities feel any need to seek consultancy assistance.

Two other problems emerged which are undoubtedly relevant to performance management of the 1990s. John Humble expected managers to contribute to the success of the MBO system by committing themselves to continuous performance improvement. He thought managers would gain personal satisfaction by achieving self-suggested objectives and that consequently there would be a motivational incentive for managers to set themselves higher and higher standards. While this idea has some validity, it was undermined in practice by the MBO system being used as a top management tool for assessing managers' performance and in many cases, their pay. Canny managers soon realised that if they were going to be judged on the extent to which they met their objectives, it was best to suggest objectives which they were sure they could meet. With salary increases and promotion affected by MBO records, there was a powerful disincentive to offer or agree to ambitious performance targets.

There was a related, though inverse problem for organisations which enthusiastically set themselves objectives and standards which proved difficult or impossible to achieve. Misled into thinking that intensive planning, forecasting and objective setting almost guaranteed success, these companies soon became disillusioned when unexpected events, or the inability of all their managers to cope, resulted in targets being missed. For these organisations, MBO became a way of what one chief executive described as 'legislating for failure'. Striking a sensible balance between caution and courage when setting objectives is as tricky an issue now as it ever was.

Performance management in the 1990s

Although MBO in the detailed Humble/Urwick Orr model died out after a few years, it would be wrong to think that the principles on which this system was based have also been consigned to the waste-bin. The logic of working towards the achievement of predetermined aims and objectives has been too powerful for most organisations to ignore, even if the way this is translated into operational systems may vary widely. Management by objectives in the informal sense (no capitals) never really went away, while the 1980s and 1990s saw a resurgence of formal schemes based on the principles originally enunciated by Peter Drucker. 1970s' MBO has consequently metamorphosed into 1990s' PMS – performance management systems.

A summarised comparison shows that PMS shares many features with MBO, despite the change of jargon:

MBO and PMS compared	
MBO	*PMS*
Generally a packaged system	Generally tailor-made systems
Applied only to managers	Applied to all staff
Emphasis on individual objectives	Emphasis on corporate values and goals
Emphasis on quantified performance measures	Inclusion of qualitative assessments
Jobs divided into key results areas (KRAs)	Jobs divided into accountabilities
Objectives set for each KRA	Objectives set for each accountability
Performance measures	Performance indicators
Action plans to achieve objectives	Action plans to achieve objectives
Annual goal-setting and review meeting	Annual appraisal meeting
Complex paperwork	Schemes vary in amount of documentation
Schemes 'owned' by specialists	Schemes 'owned' by managers

As this table shows, PMS shares many features with MBO, even though some of the jargon has changed. MBO divided jobs into 'key results areas' – broadly the same as 'principal accountabilities' in PMS-speak. Both systems set objectives for each segment of the job and both distinguish between task-based objectives and personal development goals. Both require the identification of performance measures and the use of annual appraisals of performance against objectives.

But there are also important differences. In full-blown PMS, the starting point is a definition of the organisation's mission and core values – a cultural element not found in MBO. The application of MBO was generally restricted to managers, whereas PMS is applicable to all employees. In most PMS schemes there is a greater recognition of qualitative performance indicators (such as customer satisfaction ratings) than in MBO. PMS tends to be led by chief executives and top management teams and not, as for many MBO initiatives, by personnel or management services specialists. There is much less reliance in PMS on proprietary systems bought off-the-shelf from consultants. In general, the PMS approach is more comprehensive and strategically focused than MBO and may, therefore, stand a better chance of survival.

It would be unwise, however, to think that because of its beneficial differences from MBO, PMS will take root as a permanent best way of securing a high level of organisational and individual performance. Some schemes are drifting back into an over-emphasis on financial and cost-cutting objectives. The benefits of appraisal systems are being undermined by their use to determine performance payments. Too much reliance is being placed on objective setting and review as an annual event, overlooking the fact that tying the performance management activity to a single annual date is patently absurd in today's fast-moving and unpredictable world. Schemes are being introduced without sufficient thought as to whether their style is compatible with the organisational culture. Some schemes have become administratively complex with lengthy appraisal forms and multi-page manuals of instructions. No confident prognosis is possible. Some schemes are likely to succeed and become, in effect, their organisation's natural way of managing. The 'scheme' – a term which implies a discrete activity – will become the company style. Others can be guaranteed to fail: their over-emphasis on the process as an end in itself, or their incompatibility with the prevailing culture, are the seeds of their own destruction.

Performance management in local government

Unlike MBO, which was closely identified with one guru (John Humble), performance management systems have not been promoted by any single, named academic or consultant in either the private or public sector. Hay Management Consultants have certainly been heavily involved in advising on the introduction of one particular approach, with Cambridge County Council one of the earliest local authority users of this system. But other authorities have evolved their own systems, and other consultants than Hay have also been involved.

Recently however, the Audit Commission's 'People , Pay and Performance' study has given the subject considerable prominence, with the Commission acting rather like a corporate guru with constitutional clout in its promotion of the PMS approach set out in its hefty 1995 performance management manual.[1] Effective performance management, in the Commission's view and as defined in its manual, consists of:

> "Six separate functions which can be combined into a PM strategy based upon three processes covering both individual and organisational aspects of performance management".

The three processes, each with two elements, are:
- Specification:
  — a set of financially realistic aims and objectives, cascaded down the authority from the corporate level to that of the individual employee;
  — a business planning process additional to the annual budget cycle.
- Communication:
  — external communication to help define objectives responsive to the needs of the public;
  — internal communication to ensure staff understand their responsibilities and role in contributing to the formulation and implementation of policy.
- Evaluation:
  — performance review, to monitor the performance of departments and units;
  — personal appraisal, to monitor the performance of individual employees.

The manual stresses that these processes must form an integrated whole, must be given a strong corporate lead – "normally from the chief executive and head of personnel" – and involve a degree of formality to ensure systems are in place to make it all happen. The Commission acknowledges that many authorities are developing systematic performance management but comments that, as yet, few councils have fully integrated systems in place.

The manual does not put forward a model system, and accepts that each authority needs to develop an approach consistent with its own culture and values. It provides some useful warnings against tendencies which could lead to PMS being little more than an irrelevant, time-consuming or cosmetic process. It also advises against setting unrealistic objectives which are soon ignored because they represent little more than a wish list. "Objectives", says the Commission, "must be funded, which means developing them from a business planning framework". The manual distinguishes between aims – statements of intentions – and objectives – targeted outcomes. Two examples – one corporate, one for an individual library manager are:

- **Corporate aim:** To improve the town centre environment.
- **Corporate objective:** To produce a pedestrianisation plan of the High Street within a budget of £X by ...date...
- **Individual aim:** To ensure the effective provision of information about town centre events within the town centre library.
- **Individual objective:** To implement a system for the systematic collection and display of information about forthcoming events by ...date...

Borrowing from other sources, the manual uses the acronym SMART to describe the characteristics of effectively defined objectives, i.e. **specific, measurable, agreed, realistic, timebound.** It also suggests that objectives can be of four main types:

- **Quantitative:** e.g. To reduce the number of administrative support staff from X to Y.
- **Financial:** e.g. To reduce the average cost per building control inspection to £A.
- **Qualitative:** e.g. To obtain external recognition for the quality of a specified service (e.g. a Chartermark, ISO 9000, IIP etc.)
- **Timebound:** e.g. To produce a report for council on economic development by ...date...

The Commission places much importance on the review stage of the whole performance management process – beginning with the implementation of systems and the use of performance indicators to ensure elected members have the information they need to monitor how the authority and each service is performing. As with objectives, performance indicators (PIs) are seen as cascaded from the corporate to individual level. Using a checklist developed by Redditch Borough Council, the manual suggests councils should ask of each PI:

- Is it relevant? Does it provide a useful guide to efficiency and effectiveness?
- Is it measurable? Can the target or standard be quantified in some way?

- Is it pure? Does it really measure what it seems to indicate?
- Is it realistic? Can standards be achieved?
- Does it reflect the authority's core values and policy objectives?

The nearest the manual comes to suggesting a specific system is in the personal appraisal stage which it says should apply to all staff – not just managers. Emphasising that appraisals should consider both job performance and employees' training and career development needs, the manual sets out a number of principles for the conducting of appraisal discussions between managers and their staff:

- Appraisals should consider past and current performance, and set objectives for the future.
- The appraisal should address job performance and the employee's skills and competence.
- Objectives should be evolved jointly between each employee and his or her manager.
- Appraisal should be two-way discussions, with employees contributing ideas for improvement and views about support which might be needed from their managers.
- For every objective there should be an action plan indicating how the objective will be achieved.
- Administration and paperwork should be kept to a minimum.
- Appraisals should not include discussion or consideration of performance pay.
- Senior management and the personnel function should monitor the whole process to ensure consistency and identify matters requiring corporate attention.

Although this advice stops short of suggesting a detailed appraisal procedure, it would be only a short step to design an annual appraisal programme (including a set of forms) based on these principles. Many authorities have already implemented performance appraisal schemes which comply with the Commission's guidelines – though a number would rightly be criticised by the Commission as treating appraisal as a largely self-contained activity, driven by the personnel function, and involving too much documentation and form-filling. Some authorities' approach to performance management is much closer to failed MBO than to the holistic thrust of the Commission's concept of PMS.

The Commission sees performance management as an integrated approach to the totality of management, linking strategic policy-making, business planning, objective-setting, communication, training, pay control and performance review – with employee appraisal as only one of many elements. This concept has a good deal of intellectual appeal, particularly to those who see management as an essentially logical process. It is very difficult to fault an argument that what everyone should be doing in an authority is working towards the achievement of objectives which in turn are derived from plans which support corporate and service aims and strategies in line with the authority's values and mission – QED.

The problem is putting all this into practice in a not wholly predictable political, economic, technological and social environment – and where results are dependent on the competence and commitment of people, as individuals and teams. People, unlike computers, cannot be programmed to operate consistently to pre-determined standards, and a textbook performance management system will neither generate nor guarantee the qualities of creativity, innovation and enthusiasm which distinguish the best authorities from the boringly acceptable average. There is also a significant risk that managers who are intellectually attracted by the logic of the Commission's approach will fall into the trap of treating the design and operation of the necessary formal procedures as an end in itself. The only real tests of any performance management process is whether performance improves – not whether all the appraisals have been conducted on time and all the forms have been filled in correctly.

To be fair, the Commission recognises these risks. The manual stresses the need for effective internal communication and for employees to be informed, involved and trained. It refers to the influence of organisational culture and provides an example, from Fareham Borough Council, of a cultural review. The importance of employee morale and motivation was recognised in the People, Pay and Performance study by the use of an attitude survey in a sample of 17 authorities which showed a statistically significant link between constructive staff attitudes and comprehensive performance management.

The manual also provides evidence of considerable sensitivity by the Commission to possible criticism about its approach implying the introduction of new forms of bureaucracy. Almost every suggestion about the need for systematic and defined procedures is qualified by statements such as a warning against 'descending into routine ticking of boxes', treating the use of PIs as 'an academic exercise', and producing 'a triumph of procedure over substance'. After stating that a structured approach is necessary and commending the use of a whole range of specific and defined procedures, the manual says: "Councils should formalise the PM process as little as possible". It goes on to describe four ways in which councils can "reduce the administrative burden of performance management" – a slightly unfortunate phrase as it implies that some sort of burden is inevitable. The four ways are:

- Integrating the corporate elements of PM into the normal council, committee and management team sessions and documentation.
- Combining service and personal objectives for senior officers, because what a department or unit is targeted to achieve is coincident with the responsibility of its manager.
- Balancing formal, centralised systems with informal, decentralised systems; or beginning PMS with a centrally defined and regulated system but reducing the formality and degree of central control once the approach has taken root.
- Eliminating or avoiding duplication, by incorporating any existing processes (such as policy development and budgeting) which, either raw or modified, fit a PMS approach.

Overall, the Commission's concept of PMS does seem far more potentially effective than the more restricted and mechanistic forms of 1970s MBO. The emphasis on the linkage between all aspects of management, on the need for compatibility with values, and on the importance of managerial and employee commitment, echoes the 7-S messages described in chapter 2 – though the Commission makes no reference to this earlier concept. In practice, however, authorities have clearly found it very difficult to evolve the fully integrated approach which this version of PMS involves. There are examples of many variants in which some elements have been developed but where other elements are missing. Thus one authority has an excellent personal appraisal system but no business planning process. Another, with a well-developed business planning process, sets objectives for services and business units but not for staff. Others operate performance reviews of services but not of managers, of managers but not of staff at large – or vice versa.

The Commission, too, might benefit from taking some of its own advice about minimising formality and not adopting a tick-box approach to assessments of performance. The way some District Auditors are using the audit guide the Commission produced to support its performance management study comes perilously close to the type of activity condemned in the manual as mechanistic. These auditors are using 29 performance indicators, produced by the Commission, to assess the standard of authorities' people, pay and performance management processes. These PIs include a number of statistical indices – such as the percentage of posts on pay scales 1 and 2 and staff per 1,000 population. Auditors compare each authority's figures with the average for broadly similar authorities and seem to assume that any significant variation is either good or bad – depending on the nature of the variation. Other PIs are simply factual – e.g. has the authority got a mission statement and corporate objectives: yes or no. Yes is good. No is bad.

This type of simplistic assessment is tick-boxing at its worst as it wholly fails to consider the quality of the factors it is checking. A mission statement might be unadulterated eyewash and the corporate objectives no more than best wishes – yet the fact that they have been written may earn an approving tick of the auditor's green pen. What the audit process fails to examine is whether whatever performance management processes the authority operates are actually achieving improvements in performance. And authority performance in terms of service delivery and the council's effectiveness as a voice for the local community cannot be measured by making statistical comparisons of the rates of staff sickness absence or the average paybill per full-time equivalent (to quote two more of the 29 PIs). To borrow a quote from the manual, some may well think that the Commission's approach in some of its studies – not only in the people, pay and performance context – is in danger of being "a triumph of procedure over substance". And that is what sunk MBO in the 1970s.

Footnotes:
1. *Paying the Piper...Calling the Tune. People, Pay and Performance in Local Government. A management handbook.* Audit Commission, 1995.

Chapter 6

Empowerment and the psychological contract

'Empowerment' is one of the most widely used and least clearly defined management buzzwords of the 1990s. The term seems to have had its origins in other fields than business management, being used by feminist writers and sociologists to describe antidotes to the powerlessness of traditionally disadvantaged groups in society. Used in this context, the emphasis has been on providing the individuals or groups concerned with the rights and resources – the power – to further their own interests. In the management context, while the idea of providing employees with more powers of action and decision seems similar, the business objective is to further the interests of the organisation. Hence, some of the trade union cynicism about managers who claim to have empowered their staff to decide how they want to work. Empowerment in this sense can be seen to be severely limited to the freedom to act in ways which benefit the employer.

Rosabeth Moss Kanter: power and powerlessness

Although no one management guru can be said to have been solely responsible for developing the concept of empowerment in the world of business and employment, by far the most influential writer on the subject has been the Harvard professor, Rosabeth Moss Kanter. By training she is a sociologist, and her ideas about empowerment grew out of her largely sociological study in the mid 1970s of people's roles in large organisations. At that time, her interest, in her own words, "was in demonstrating how differences in where individuals stood in the organisation, by virtue of their job design and location, affected their access to power".

This study led to her first book, *Men and Women of the Corporation*, published in 1977, in which she concluded that most organisations were failing to tap into the potential talent of their staff – particularly their women employees. The book suggested that organisations should open up their promotion channels to a far wider range of candidates – particularly women and workers in 'powerless' first-line jobs, and that flatter management hierarchies and self-managed work groups were needed to achieve a wider and more effective distribution of power.

Perhaps because the book was seen more as an interesting social study with an equal opportunity bias than as a business management text, it did not lead at that time to any great upsurge of interest in empowerment by business managers. This had to await her second book in 1983, *The Change Masters*. By this time, Moss Kanter could draw on her experience as a business consultant and on her growing knowledge of Japanese and other non-American companies, and the book was acknowledged as a major contribution to management literature. One influential reviewer in the States described it as "of immeasurably higher quality than the best-selling *In Search of Excellence*" – while Tom Peters himself was gracious enough to describe her third major book, *When Giants Learn to Dance* (published in 1989) as "the benchmark against which management books of the 90s are measured". (This book is not discussed here as it is concerned primarily with giant multi-national corporations operating in a global marketplace.)

The Change Masters put empowerment firmly on the management map. The book compared the characteristics of innovative companies which fostered an entrepreneurial spirit among their staff with those of companies Moss Kanter described as 'change resisters'. Running through the whole book is the theme that companies need to develop an 'integrative' rather than 'segmented' approach – linking all their functions, harnessing creative thinking at all levels and distributing widely the power to innovate in response to threats and opportunities.

(By segmentation she meant the rigid separation of functions, narrowly defined jobs, and powerful status distinctions between different management levels. She used two phrases to encapsulate the characteristics of the integrative organisation – 'participative management' and, of course, empowerment.

In view of the limited interpretation of empowerment by some UK consultants (for example, that it is mainly concerned with job enlargement), it is important to recognise that Moss Kanter's concept is extremely wide. She sees empowerment as something permeating the whole organisation and deriving from fundamental cultural change. To quote:

> "The degree to which the opportunity to use power effectively is granted to or withheld from individuals is one operative difference between those companies which stagnate and those which innovate. The difference begins with a company's approach to problem-solving and extends throughout its culture and structure".[1]

She also links empowerment with the existence of a comprehensive range of progressive employment policies, such as affirmative action programmes for women and ethnic minorities, employee participation schemes, and systems of rewards which encourage innovative future action rather than simply paying for past performance. Any managers who think that the benefits of empowerment can be achieved simply by providing staff on the front desk of one-stop shops with sufficient information to be able to answer most callers' questions is in for a shock if they read *The Change Masters*. What Moss Kanter called for in that book and in *When Giants Learn to Dance* is a complete revolution in how large organisations are organised and behave – not a few cosmetic changes to basic grade job descriptions.

She sees power as deriving from three 'basic commodities':

- Information – including conventional management data, technical know-how, and political intelligence – meaning organisational, not party, politics.
- Resources – including money, materials and time.
- Support – in terms of endorsement, backing and approval.

It is an individual's access to these three commodities which determines how much power they have to make decisions and innovate. She goes on to describe three broad aspects of the way innovative organisations operate to secure the necessary enlarged 'power circulation and power access'. These are:

- Open communication systems – making it easy for people to approach each other across functional boundaries and throughout the management hierarchy to seek information or support, or to exchange ideas.
- Network-forming arrangements – to help people build 'coalitions of supporters'.
- Decentralisation of resources – to ensure that funds, equipment or time are available to match people's decision-making freedoms.

The Change Masters places a lot of emphasis on the second of these aspects – effective networking – and suggests there are four particular devices which organisations can use to foster the formation of networks:

- Frequent mobility, with managers in particular transferring sideways from function to function at quite frequent intervals. It does not then take many moves for a group of staff who have worked together to be dispersed around the organisation so that each has a colleague in another section to contact for information or support.
- Security of employment – the expectation of a continued place in the organisation, not only for oneself but for colleagues in the network
- Team-working – partly because this has a direct value in pooling ideas and expertise but also because multi-functional teams help individuals create on-going personal contacts in other functions than their own.
- 'Complex ties permitting cross-cutting access' – an unusually clumsy phrase for a normally very clear writer. It involves the acceptance of apparently complicated organisational relationships such as a manager reporting to different senior managers for different aspects of his or her job, matrix working with project teams being formed and reformed as circumstances require, and an acceptance that many working contacts can be made which cut across the lines and boxes on the formal organisation chart.

Moss Kanter recognised that most of the ideas just outlined applied primarily to the empowerment of middle managers, and that the freedom for managers to innovate did not automatically extend to what she termed the organisation's foot soldiers. She consequently developed the empowerment concept in a chapter of *The Change Masters* entitled *Energizing the grass roots*. The challenge, as she described it, is to combine the necessity for routine jobs with the creation of opportunities for employee participation beyond these jobs. Her solution was to form a parallel organisation, in which a formally constituted system of workers and managers in egalitarian, problem-solving teams or task forces, operates alongside the conventional day-to-day organisation structure. She stresses that the involvement of employees in the problem-solving or 'organic' organisation must be recognised as being as real and important as the operational structure. To quote:

> "An innovating organisation needs at least two organisations, two ways of arraying and using its people. It needs a hierarchy with specified tasks and functional grouping for carrying out what it already knows how to do... But it also needs a set of flexible vehicles for figuring out how to do what it does not yet know – ... engaging the grass roots as well as the elite in the mastery of innovation and change".[2]

Given this very radical view, it is not surprising that she questions whether what some managers would see as empowerment – such as quality circles or initiatives to make routine jobs more interesting – can really be considered as empowerment as they do little or nothing to change the distribution of real power in an organisation.

The psychological contract

Moss Kanter's writings on empowerment have become linked in recent years with those of another American sociologist, Edgar Schein. His major contribution to organisational theory was to develop the concept of organisational or corporate culture – the subject of the next chapter. But he is also credited with coining the term 'the psychological contract' to describe the mutual assumptions and expectations which influence the relationship between an organisation and its staff. The link with empowerment is that employees will not behave in the committed, innovative manner which Rosabeth Moss Kanter describes unless there is mutual trust between them and their employer – and mutuality is a contract principle.

In fact, the first guru to discuss the psychology of the employer/employee relationship in ways which parallel empowerment theories was Chris Argyris, an American organisational psychologist. His 1973 book, *Management: Tasks, Responsibilities, Practices*, was based on the idea that every manager has a potential which can either flourish or wilt depending on the organisational environment. Argyris pointed out that much of the commitment by an employer towards the employees – and vice versa – was implicit and not spelled out in formal terms. To put this another way, the formal, legal contract of employment spells out what the employee has to do: the psychological contract determines how well the employee does it.

Edgar Schein developed these ideas, using the term 'psychological contract', beginning with his book, *Career Dynamics: Matching Individual and Organisational Needs*, published in 1978. The title highlights the idea of a mutuality of interest between an organisation and its staff. Describing this as a contract is a reminder that each party has expectations of the other which need to be met if the relationship is to work well. The organisation looks to the employee for loyalty and commitment: the employee looks to the organisation for recognition and support.

This concept has attracted particular attention in recent years because many organisations consider they are unable to offer the type of implicit benefits to their staff which were considered in the past to be vital in securing employees' loyalty and commitment. The most obvious change relates directly to one of the four preconditions which Moss Kanter thought were needed to develop productive internal relationships – security of employment. Partly because of a more turbulent economic and commercial environment, partly because of the fashionable concept of the flexible organisation (see chapter 8), many organisations in the public and private sectors now state openly that the idea of lifetime careers with one employer is dead. Other changes include less predictable salaries as a result of performance-related pay and the transfer of 'ownership' of career development from the organisation to the individual. Taken together, many of the changes in employment policies and practices encapsulated in the concept of human resource management could be thought to undermine staff loyalty and discourage innovation. Why bother to come up with new ideas or risk sticking your neck out by questioning current working practices if you might well be made redundant next month, or reduce your performance bonus by abandoning a working routine you are good at?

Few organisations have yet produced wholly convincing answers to this dilemma. Even Tom Peters, one of the most fervent exponents of organisational flexibility, has recently expressed doubts. Referring to the large-scale growth in the use of temporary staff, he says: "How do you instil loyalty and the company's culture in someone who's only going to be with you for a few months? How do you get people to put out 110% when they know they're only involved for the short term?"[3] His rather glib answer – "Never treat a temp like a temp!" is not very convincing.

There are two responses which have some merit and are not in conflict with empowerment theory. The first is that while an organisation may not be able to offer long term employment it can act positively to help its staff improve their employability. Offering opportunities for acquiring a breadth of experience – particularly in new technologies – and supporting employees' own self-development programmes can be seen by staff as a positive benefit which offsets job insecurity. Moss Kanter's suggestion that the organisation benefits from managers' quite frequent job changes can also be seen to benefit the managers by broadening their range of know-how. The second and related factor is the provision of interesting and psychologically rewarding work or ways of working. For most managers and staff at large, working in an organisation structured and operating as Moss Kanter recommends is a more personally satisfying experience than working within the compartmentalised and closely controlled environment of the conventional bureaucracy. But whether these approaches are enough to outweigh the downside of employment in the flexible organisation has yet to be proved. The essence of a good contract is that the two parties see its benefits as reasonably equally allocated, and in the psychological contract, employers cannot dictate employees' perceptions in the same way as they can generally dictate the terms of the legal contract of employment.

Implications for local authorities

Before accepting every word of Rosabeth Moss Kanter's persuasive arguments about the nature and benefits of empowerment, it should be remembered that the underlying issue she was addressing was the diminishing world competitiveness of American companies – not the challenges facing UK local authorities at the end of the 1990s. Her concern was with the type of organisational culture which could foster the qualities needed for survival and success in a fiercely competitive commercial environment. Despite CCT and market testing, local authorities are far more stable entities than even the most successful companies, which can be wiped out by takeovers or the emergence of an aggressive rival. One of the most frequently used words in all Moss Kanter's books is innovation. While local authorities as well as companies benefit from a continuous flow of new ideas, continuity and certainty also have significant relevance in the provision of public services.

There are two other reasons specific to public services why local authorities may not be able to go as far as commercial companies in devolving decision-making authority and resources (i.e. power) to individual managers or down to lower organisational levels:

- Some decisions which affect the liberty or safety of people – such as taking a child into care – are too serious and sensitive to be made solely by one person.
- Local authorities are publicly accountable for their use of public money, and it is not acceptable for them to incur the same degree of financial risk as an innovative and entrepreneurial company might take.

Within constraints of these kinds, there is still scope for a local authority to develop a number of the ideas within the concepts of empowerment and the psychological contract.

The first and fairly modest point relates to delegation. The idea that good managers are good delegators is not, of course, a new management concept. It has been around for decades, even though many managers have difficulty putting it into practice. Managers may think they are effective delegators, but subordinate staff will say that the only tasks which get delegated are those the manager does not want to do – not necessarily the tasks the subordinate staff could do best. Managers may also find difficulty striking a balance between letting go and maintaining some influence or control. In the words of Rosabeth Moss Kanter:

"Some managers assume an either/or world where they are either in complete control or they have given up all control. But delegation… means that the manager not only sets the basic conditions but also stays involved".

By involvement she means being available to give advice and support, and to review progress and results – not interference with the task actually being done.

Although conventional delegation is not full-blooded empowerment in the Moss Kanter sense, the principles of effective delegation and empowerment are exactly the same and have become more important as a result of three increasingly common organisational changes:

- The simplification of organisation structures ('de-layering'): when whole tiers of management or supervision are stripped out, most of the displaced work is shifted down to lower levels. Are they equipped to handle this increased responsibility?
- The devolution of decision-making to more independent 'business units': the managers of these units have generally been given authority (power) to make many decisions about purchasing, personnel and operational procedures which traditionally have been reserved for central, senior management. Again, have they been equipped to cope effectively?
- The emphasis on customer care: this has resulted in the redesign and enlargement of many front-line jobs to enable citizens and service users to obtain information and advice from a single source. The same question arises – how well can they cope?

Drawn from *The Change Masters*, there is a three element checklist to apply whenever any organisational changes are made along the lines just outlined. For the managers or staff to whom more work has been delegated or more authority devolved:

- Have they been provided with all the information they need? Not just narrowly to handle the operational detail of the tasks involved, but also contextual information about how their new tasks fit into the authority's corporate and service strategies, which of the authority's values are of particular importance and, if relevant, any political implications.
- Have they the resources needed to undertake the tasks effectively? This is not only a matter of equipment or finance, but also that very important and often under-rated resource – time. Too often, additional tasks are delegated to staff whose time is already fully occupied with other work.
- Will they be given adequate support? Particularly in the early stages of taking on new and more complex or responsible work, the staff concerned may need guidance and coaching to develop the necessary know-how. Additionally, there may be some reluctance on the part of other staff (and perhaps service users) to accept that their contacts will now be with staff at a lower level. When people have been used to dealing directly with a chief officer or other senior manager, they may feel the importance of their functions or concerns has been diminished by now having to contact the staff to whom the work has been devolved. In this situation, the senior manager owes it to his or her staff to explain and support the delegated arrangements – not to be apologetic or fudge the delegation by continuing to deal directly with anyone who complains.

There is another awkward point which cannot or should not be ducked – pay. Staff may be very willing to take on additional responsibility and enjoy the challenge and improved job satisfaction this involves. But if the change is significant, they will almost certainly feel this should be reflected in their rates of pay. Those white-collar staff whose contracts of employment import the terms of national agreements – and they are still the majority – will quote paragraph 80 of the Purple Book (the compendium of national agreements). This gives employees the right of appeal if their pay grade is not improved when there has been "a substantial change in the duties and responsibilities of the post" which goes beyond variations in duties which do not change "the general character of the duties or the level of responsibility entailed".

An authority which is enthusiastic about the simplification of its management structure and the devolution of responsibilities to the lowest possible level (in other words, an empowerment strategy) needs to play fair with its staff by not attempting to obtain the benefits of such a strategy on the cheap. Both the legal and psychological contracts are involved. Legally, employees have a contractual right to have their pay grades reassessed in these circumstances. Psychologically, empowerment strategies will generate cynicism and a lack of commitment if employees perceive all the benefits as one-sided.

The other principal application of empowerment and psychological contract theories is related to how authorities organise their frequent studies and reviews of various aspects of their activities. Changes in legislation, finance, technology or public expectations, frequently require authorities to review and revise policies and practices at both the corporate and service levels. Authorities are consequently often setting up project teams or working parties to study specific issues and produce proposals for change. Conventionally, the membership of such teams is limited to a few senior managers or professionals who are already recognised as being particularly knowledgeable about the relevant subject matter. While it is obviously sensible to involve the necessary experts, project studies of this kind provide a rich opportunity to involve a much wider range of know-how and ideas – particularly from the probably lower-graded front-line staff. For example, an authority which decides its payroll function needs a fundamental redesign might conventionally allocate this task to a team of just three people – the senior accountant to whom the payroll supervisor reports, an IT specialist and a management services officer. They would talk to the payroll supervisor and some of the payroll clerks, but that would be the limit of these staff's involvement. An alternative approach, influenced by empowerment theory, would be to place the responsibility for the redesign of the system on the payroll section itself – with the involvement of specialists such as an IT expert and a cost accountant being seen as the provision of resources to a payroll team. At this point, traditionalists will probably throw up their hands in horror, asserting that the payroll section will only be concerned with preserving or increasing its own status, or that payroll clerks are not sufficiently bright to be able to produce innovative ideas. Managers who think this way need to be reminded of two things:

- The staff actually doing a task generally know far more about it than anyone more senior, and often have ideas about how it could be improved.
- The primary quality needed in exercises of this kind, in addition to any obviously necessary specialist know-how, is common sense. There is no evidence that this quality is distributed other than evenly throughout the population.

In many cases, the membership of a study or project team needs to be drawn more widely than simply from the staff currently directly involved. For example, if a leisure department is reviewing its customer complaints procedures, it could benefit from the ideas of a working party which included one or two staff from other departments where complaints procedures are considered to be working well. Here, too, the inclusion of operational staff – say a pool attendant and a leisure centre receptionist – would be of advantage.

Taking every opportunity, in parallel with normal job routines, to involve operational staff as well as managers and professionals in all kinds of studies and projects is directly in line with Rosabeth Moss Kanter's ideas, and has two particular benefits:

- The authority draws on a wider range of knowledge and experience, and proposals produced with the involvement of staff who will have to operate them helps to ensure both their practicability and successful implementation.
- Over time, the authority builds up a stock of staff who, through their involvement in project work, have developed a wider understanding of services and their own abilities, and are therefore a more potentially capable and flexible workforce.

In terms of the psychological contract, if it is accepted that one element in the employer's obligations is to help staff improve their employability, then involvement in project teams can certainly be seen as a contributory factor. Operational employees who can list their experience in several such studies on their CVs should have the edge over those with no such experience if at some stage – perhaps as a result of unavoidable redundancy – they need to seek work elsewhere.

Authorities which pay regard to the general theory of the psychological contract need to consider very carefully the extent to which they disband jobs involving normal open-ended contracts of employment and shift to temporary and fixed term appointments. There are certainly situations in which contracts just for the duration of a project or work peak are fully justified. But some authorities seem to have followed a private sector trend of using temporary staff and fixed term employment simply as a current fashion, rather than for any specific purpose. There are signs, too, of responsible and successful companies questioning the extent to which these insecure employment practices have been developed, so authorities which want to be in line with leading edge personnel strategies would do well to ensure they are up-to-date and not following last year's fashion.

Common sense, let alone psychological theory, indicates that staff who know their employment will soon come to an end are likely to put their own immediate and future interests a long way ahead of those of their employer. Loyalty and commitment are not one-way aims or obligations. The authority which wants a loyal and committed workforce had better accept that its side of this psychological bargain is to demonstrate loyalty and commitment to its staff.

Footnotes:
1. *The Change Masters*, Rosabeth Moss Kanter, Routledge, 1995 edition.
2. *ibid.*
3. *The Pursuit of WOW!*, Tom Peters, Macmillan, 1995 edition.

Chapter 7

Organisational culture

How the concept of culture emerged

Twenty years ago, most managers would have associated the word culture either with the arts or with a laboratory material on which to grow penicillin. Academics and management writers in the 1950s and 1960s had occasionally used the word in an organisational context, such as the well-known American consultant, Robert Blake, who commented in a book published in 1969 that "managers are prisoners of their own corporate cultures".[1] A more obscure writer, C Kluckhohn, had written an article even earlier in a Harvard publication in 1953 entitled *Dominant and Variant Cultural Value Orientations*, though no-one seemed to take much notice. In 1972 an article, by R Harrison in the Harvard Review on *Understanding your Organization's Character*, suggested that organisations could be classified as conforming to four main cultural types but, again, this aroused little managerial interest.

In 1976, Charles Handy, one of the very few British gurus to acquire international recognition, published his first book, *Understanding Organisations*, in which he said all organisations develop their own cultures, adding that to be able to work effectively in an organisation, it was necessary to join it psychologically as well as physically – an early reference to the psychological contract as well the concept of culture. The book also described four cultural categories concerned with power, roles, tasks and people, which are examined later in this chapter, and were the same four types that Harrison had described in his 1972 Harvard Review article. Handy developed his ideas about culture three years later with his most off-the-wall book yet, *The Gods of Management*, and in an updated version of *Understanding Organisations* in 1991.

However, the concept of organisational culture did not attract the full attention of managers until the 1980s. It was then given a considerable boost by what is generally stated to be the first book to provide a full discussion of culture – Edgar Schein's *Organizational Culture and Leadership*, published in 1985. Thus Carol Kennedy's very useful paperback, *Guide to the Management Gurus*, says "Schein virtually invented the concept of corporate culture". This seems a bit rough on

Harrison and Handy, although it is interesting that Handy had studied under Schein at the Sloan School of Management (Massachusetts Institute of Technology).

It was partly Schein's timing which helped to gain him recognition as the founding guru of organisational culture, and culture as a critically important concept in understanding what makes organisations tick – and why organisations differ so significantly in style and character. Prior to the mid 1980s (and at the risk of dangerous over-generalisation) it can be suggested that most organisations had either evolved their particular styles without much conscious planning, or – when they saw the need for change – attempted to achieve it by introducing new structures and systems. In 7-S terms, they concentrated on just two of the Ss – Structure and Systems – and overlooked Shared Values, Strategy, Style, Staff and Skills. Given the increasing need in the commercial sector for innovation and responsiveness to external trends, a growing number of companies in the 1980s came to realise that something more fundamental was needed than new organisation charts and revised procedure manuals. Somehow, the whole nature of the organisation and the pervasive attitudes of its managers and staff needed to change. The question arose, was it inevitable that managers were, in Blake's terms, prisoners of their organisation's culture, or could managers become cultural masters and make cultural changes? Schein's view was that such changes could be achieved and that the management of cultural change was the key to successful managerial leadership.

One of the first major British organisations to embrace this view and mount a massive, planned programme of cultural change – and call it that – was British Airways. In a book describing this programme, Denis Walker (a change consultant, previously a senior BA manager) explained:

> "When Colin Marshall took over as chief executive of BA in 1983, he saw the only possible way forward was to make the requirements of the customer pre-eminent in all aspects of the operation. 'Putting the Customer First' became the theme and the rallying call of a campaign which was to last several years and was to produce a culture change which affected all its staff, its customers and its competitors".[2]

Within this campaign, there was an emphasis on top management providing a vision, articulating a set of values and defining what Walker calls 'cultural norms'. Hard-edged structural and systems changes were essential but were linked to the softer concepts of vision and values. He commented that it was essential that all managers eventually demonstrated their commitment to the new cultural norms. If, after a programme of re-education, some managers still would not or could not accept the new values, then the company had to arrange "exiting in a way which preserves dignity and self-esteem".

There will probably be arguments – not least by Richard Branson – about the extent to which BA lives up to the very high standards and cultural norms it targeted. But setting aside any such differences of view, the fact is that perhaps for the first time, a major corporation drove through a massive set of changes which affected every part of the business and which it saw clearly as an exercise in the management of cultural change. From the mid 1980s, many other organisations have followed suit, so that 'culture' has now become a normal part of the management vocabulary. During this period, too, public sector organisations have taken the cultural concept on board, with a particular emphasis (as originally in British Airways) on changing from a traditional bureaucratic culture to one which is responsive to its users.

What is organisational culture?

Given the widespread current use of cultural terminology, it is curious that no-one has yet produced a generally accepted definition of culture. Descriptions by different gurus range from Tom Peters' and others' simplistic:

- "The way we do things around here".
- Through to the more sociological: "culture consists of an organisation's shared meanings, values, attitudes and beliefs".[3]
- To much more esoteric definitions such as: "Culture consists of patterns, explicit and implicit, of and for behaviour acquired and transmitted by symbols, constituting the distinctive achievements of human groups... The essential core of culture consists of historically derived and selected ideas and especially their attached values".[4]

Edgar Schein saw culture as a largely unconscious but all-pervasive entity, being the product of an organisation's unwritten perception of itself. This perception conditioned the attitude and behaviour of the organisation's employees and could be categorised as made up of:

- Artefacts, such as the nature and general appearance of the offices and the way staff dress.
- Values, the qualities the organisation and its people think are important – often derived from company 'mythology'.
- Assumptions about the organisation's purpose, and how it and its people should behave internally and in its external contacts.

He summarised the culture of an organisation as: "what it has learned as a total social unit over the course of its history".

Charles Handy adopted a different approach and, in *Understanding Organisations* and *The Gods of Management*, suggested that organisations can be classified according to four broad cultural types:

- **Power culture:** characterised by a strong central power source (often the founder of the business) which exercises control through a cadre of personally selected and trusted individuals. Organisations of this type operate on the basis of personal influence rather than formal procedures and are the antithesis of the public sector bureaucracy. They tend to be self-confident, fast-moving and risk-taking.
- **Role culture:** the bureaucratic organisation which operates impersonally and

rationally through defined roles and formal rules. Its characteristics are stability, consistency and caution, and it has difficulty surviving in a turbulent environment.

- **Task culture:** a matrix-type organisation or meritocracy which focuses on specific projects. Power and influence derive from expertise, rather than personality or role. It is not an easy culture to control and, while successful in specific tasks, may be unstable in the longer term.
- **Person culture:** a culture in which the prime purpose of the organisation is seen to be serving the personal interests of its people. It has no strong power structure and consists of a cluster of like-minded individuals. (Handy suggested that barristers' chambers or some small consultancies fitted this model).

In *The Gods of Management*, Handy chose four gods from Greek mythology as appropriate symbolic heads of each category. Zeus, the all-powerful thrower of thunderbolts, would head the power culture. Apollo, the god of reason, was an obvious choice as god of the role culture. Athena, the goddess of handicrafts, would head the task culture, while Dionysus would be the god of the person culture. This all seemed a tad far-fetched, particularly as Athena was better known as the goddess of war and Dionysus was also known as Bacchus, god of wine, women and song. But who knows what barristers get up to in chambers?

One of the more down-to-earth problems with Handy's approach is that it tries to slot all organisations into just four boxes, when it is not only evident that there are far more than four cultural types but also that more than one culture can exist within one organisation. County councils, for example, know all about the stark contrast in cultures between their social services departments and their fire services. Handy's work, too, though imaginative and thought-provoking, focused on cultural analysis rather than on cultural management – and the latter was what busy managers wanted to learn about.

An anthropological parallel

Before considering the practicalities of managing cultural change in a local authority context, it may be helpful to draw on a variety of sources about the nature of culture and illustrate this amalgam of ideas by using an anthropological parallel – the organisation as a tribe and the similarity of principles between organisational and tribal culture.

An anthropologist's description of tribal culture usually begins with an account of the tribe's environment and primary economic activity. Thus to understand the culture of the Masai it is necessary to know that they live on the grassy plains of East Africa and that they are cattle herders, noting, too, that cattle herding and grassy plains go together. The tribe's social structure, customs, beliefs and values all stem from its physical environment and primary activity. In the organisational parallel, the environment (whether of a company or a council) is more complex, including social, legislative, political and technological elements. But to survive, the organisation, like the successful tribe, must be fully adapted to its environment.

Organisation structure is the managerial parallel to a tribe's social structure. The principles are very similar. How, in the tribe, company or council, is authority or power distributed? To what extent are particular roles or functions specialised? There are strong links here with the nature of the primary function and the shape of the structure. The peripatetic life of the Masai does not require or support large, complex communities, nor can tribal authority be vested in a powerful, central autocracy. The Masai's social structure consists of a relatively loose-knit collection of small units with widely distributed decision-making powers. Larger tribal gatherings occur only infrequently, though they are important in reinforcing overall tribal identity, beliefs and values. Many companies have come to grief through retaining structures which are no longer compatible with the changing needs of the business. The firm which retains a rigid, centralist structure when moving from a stable to a fast-moving and highly competitive market is on the road to failure.

Tribal rules, customs and practices equate to an organisation's systems and procedures, though this can be complicated by the existence of both formal and informal systems – particularly when the formal procedures no longer meet the organisation's real requirements. The very marked feature of tribal customs and practices – 'the way they do things' – is that they reinforce the types of behaviour necessary for the tribe's survival. A key question for any organisation is whether its internal rules and regulations and its formal systems and procedures work for or against the way it needs its people to behave. In a local authority setting, for example, it has not been unusual to find formal rules and procedures in place which militate against a council's declared objectives of responsiveness and customer care. The 'caring council' which, by following the rules, prosecuted an 85 year old widower dying of cancer for £25 poll tax arrears is an extreme example.

An important aspect of anthropological study is the examination of the tribe's beliefs and values. What are the qualities the tribe considers important? For the Masai, physical strength and courage are dominant values for the obvious reason that these are essential attributes for protecting cattle against marauding lions and for surviving in small groups on the open African plains. The anthropologist will also look for the symbols, customs, myths and stories which reflect and reinforce tribal values and beliefs. For the Masai, the lion is a symbol of strength while initiation ceremonies focus on the qualities of bravery and stoicism. (In West Africa, a very different tribal culture based on more complex communities and on trading as a major activity, has cleverness as a primary value with a spider as a dominant symbol).

The organisational parallel is, of course, the organisation's values and the way these are promoted. Much of the current thinking about organisational culture focuses on the importance of values, which were discussed in detail in chapter 2, though the need for values to be reinforced by various means is worth additional comment. In the tribal context, tribal leaders do not issue value statements. Values are implicit, not explicit, but are promoted very effectively through a whole range of activities. Legends and tribal myths emphasise the importance of particular qualities or types of behaviour. The tribe's mythological founder strangles the strongest lion with one hand: the weak but clever spider outwits the strong but stupid snake. Games, ceremonies and artefacts reflect values and beliefs. The tribe's leaders or elders provide role models – they demonstrate the nature and importance of values through personal behaviour.

In organisations, values may be formally defined and publicised, but unless there are supporting activities they may be little more than words on pieces of paper. Edgar Schein saw this as a primary leadership function, or as another management writer (Andrew Pettigrew) once put it: "The leader not only creates the rational and tangible aspects of organisations such as structure and technology, but is also the creator of symbols, ideologies, language, beliefs, rituals and myths". Most organisations have a stock of stories about past events and personalities and may have 'rituals' such as an annual open day or performance award ceremony. There are also cultural symbols such as the categories of company cars or the style of the staff restaurant. Do these myths, rituals and symbols support or undermine the organisation's targeted values? In the tribe, they do – not because anyone has consciously planned them but because they have been an integral, natural and necessary element in the tribe's historic evolution.

In the organisation – company or council – the values and supporting mythology may also evolve over time without formal definition or direction. The problem is that organisational environments move too fast for this evolutionary process to keep pace – just as the rapidity of technological, demographic and political change in East Africa and elsewhere is threatening the survival of traditional tribal identities. This is the main and highly significant difference between tribal and organisational culture. In both cases, culture compatible with environment and function is central to survival. But while the development of tribal culture is unconscious, evolutionary and slow, organisations need consciously to plan and manage cultural change to keep pace with their rapidly changing environments.

Managing cultural change in local authorities
The need for changes of culture among local authorities has been caused, in the main, by three external influences:

- CCT has required at least those services involved to adopt a style which is closer to the entrepreneurial, profit-focused commercial culture than to that of the conventional cautious, even if well-intentioned, public sector bureaucracy.
- A combination of factors leading to an emphasis throughout the private and public sectors on the concepts of quality and customer care, has required a change from the traditional impersonal style and emphasis on administrative rectitude, to a more personalised and user-friendly approach.
- The rapidity and scale of a whole range of changes – legislative, economic, demographic and social – has generated a need for local authorities to develop characteristics of flexibility and responsiveness which could not be achieved in the traditional public sector culture, with its emphasis on precedent and stability.

Although these influences overlap and interact, the change from a public service to a commercial culture can be seen most clearly in the way some DSOs have all but broken away from their parent authorities in terms of identity and style. One early example of a DSO embarking on a planned programme of cultural change was described in detail in a book published by the then Institute of Personnel Management (now the Institute of Personnel and Development) in 1989 – *Changing Culture*, by Allan Williams, Paul Dobson and Mike Walters. The book included eight case studies, seven in the private sector and one in a local government – Hampshire County Council's highways maintenance DSO. This DSO programme included an integrated set of changes to the DSO's structure, working systems, staff training, employee communications, reward strategies and management style, together with symbolic developments such as the use of a DSO logo and a new identity as 'Hampshire Works'.

A significant feature of this example was its overt description as a cultural change programme, with an early management awayday examining the concept of culture as a preliminary to deciding what changes were needed. As a consequence, attention was paid to all the elements of culture described earlier in this chapter – in effect, the cultural implications of 7-S plus some specifics such as symbols. The whole process also began to generate its own mythology, with stories about who said what at various meetings and accounts of early successes and disasters. The result, to quote from the book, was: "The general feeling within the authority seems to be that the development of a distinct culture within the DSO has been remarkably successful".

However, two particular problems which were experienced in the course of the programme illustrate that achieving effective cultural change is not a quick or easy task. One was a reaction to the nature and rapidity of change from other parts of the authority. As the case study put it: "The organisation was perceived from outside as too aggressive and insular, operating to objectives which were not in accord with the culture of the authority in general". Interestingly, the DSO's reaction to this criticism was that the problem had arisen, not because the DSO had gone too far, but because other departments had not taken similar action. The two points of principle are:

- To what extent an authority should develop a wholly consistent corporate culture, as distinct from allowing different units to develop cultures of their own?
- How far should units which are in real commercial competition be allowed to develop cultures based on purely commercial, as distinct from public service, values?

These are questions each authority must decide for itself – there are no universally agreed answers.

The second problem experienced in the Hampshire case study was that senior managers latched onto the cultural objectives and action plans much more rapidly than middle managers and staff at large. In one training exercise halfway through the programme, staff were asked to draw pictures of how they then envisaged the

DSO. One section manager drew a sailing ship caught up in a storm. Up in the crow's nest was the senior management team congratulating themselves that they could see the distant harbour. Down below was everyone else, lashing down the hatches, pumping out the bilges and generally working desperately to prevent the ship sinking. A recognition of this problem led to more time and effort being given to staff training, briefing, communication and involvement – even though the importance of these aspects of cultural change had been recognised from the start.

It has been the experience of other organisations, including some local authorities, that senior managers and operational staff have been more enthusiastic about cultural change than middle management. Derek Walker commented on this in his description of the British Airways programme and his advice is relevant to any type of organisation and to cultural change aimed at customer care as well as commercialism:

> "The biggest hurdle is often the middle management group... being threatened by the changing nature of their role, feeling increasingly isolated and fearful of the future... This particular hurdle can only be overcome by leadership from the senior team, providing clear championing of 'customer first' and role modelling quality behaviour".[5]

In the Audit Commission's performance management handbook referred to earlier in chapter 5, there is the comment that: "Councils are facing increasing pressures to become externally responsive and internally flexible" – a recognition that cultural change is being driven by a wider range of influences than the specifics of CCT or customer care. These influences, which include a greater public expectation of quality, choice and helpfulness, require attention to every aspect of an authority's activities – beginning with the definition of its dominating values as discussed in chapter 2. This wide-ranging and essentially corporate approach must affect the whole authority, not as in the Hampshire case study only single units. The issues which are likely to require attention can be illustrated by the cultural review, used by Fareham Borough Council and produced in a condensed version in the Audit Commission's handbook. It is given here in its fuller, original form, as produced by the author of this book while working with Fareham on a consultancy basis.

The review consists of pairs of characteristics. Used as a review tool and to generate discussion about the need for cultural change, managers are first asked to give their authority marks out of 10 for each pair of characteristics – from a score of one if they think the authority currently fully matches the left-hand description to 10 for fully matching the right-hand description. They are then asked to give a mark for what they think the authority should aim to be in, say, a year's time. After a year of a change programme, the review can be re-scored to assess managers' perceptions of the extent to which targeted progress has been achieved.

The static organisation	The adaptable organisation
• Unresponsive to external influences.	Very responsive to external influences.
• Reaction to external change is defensive.	Reaction to external changes is opportunistic.
• Fails to identify trends in external pressures and takes action only when this is unavoidable.	Spots trends early and takes action before being forced to by circumstances.
• No regular action to monitor customer needs and views.	Constant monitoring of customer needs and views.
• Reluctance to form joint working relationships with outside bodies.	Enthusiasm for collaborative working with outside bodies
• No clear and articulated vision of role and long term objectives.	Clear and articulated vision of role and long term objectives.
• Internal focus on adherence to own rules and procedures	External focus and emphasis on action to respond to threats and opportunities
• High value placed on precedent: 'How did we do this last time?'.	Enthusiasm for fresh thinking: 'What do we want to achieve this time?'.
• Action driven from the top in a multi-level hierarchy.	Clear direction from the top on core values and corporate goals, but considerable devolution of decision-making throughout a flat management structure.
• Centralised systems of vetting and approval.	Central vetting and approval limited to minimum needed to ensure achievement of corporate goals.
• Structure reflects and supports professional groups and interests.	Structure reflects customer groupings and needs.
• Work kept strictly within formal and permanent organisational sections.	Extensive use made of inter-disciplinary project teams which are disbanded on project completion.
• Lengthy formal process for making even minor staffing or structural changes.	Considerable flexibility to make staffing and organisational changes.
• Detailed and prescriptive procedure manuals and job descriptions.	Outline procedures and job descriptions only, emphasising end purposes.
• Detailed rules and regulations governing every aspect of working life.	Rules and regulations limited to those necessary to maintain key standards and core values.
• Comprehensive documentation: managers communicate by memo.	Minimal documentation: managers communicate face-to-face.
• Reluctance to depart from formal rules or procedures: compliance an end in itself.	Readiness to alter or depart from rules or procedures which inhibit achievement of goals.
• Intolerance of mistakes: when things go wrong: 'Who is to blame?'.	Tolerance of mistakes which result from well-intentioned initiatives: when things go wrong: 'What can we learn?'
• Emphasis on 100% accuracy.	'Roughly right' often good enough provided goals are achieved.
• Reluctance to innovate in case things go wrong	Innovation positively encouraged.
• Little attempt to tap ideas/initiative of junior or front-line staff.	Active involvement of, and consultation with, all employees.
• Training mainly consists of formal courses for professional qualifications.	Emphasis is on learning from a wide variety of experiences.
• Strong sense of status distinctions.	Minimisation of status distinctions.
• Little attention to internal communication; employees poorly informed.	Extensive internal communication strategy; all employees well-informed.
• Little understanding or discussion of concepts of culture or organisational development.	Conscious attention to culture and organisational development.

While this review tool does not include every factor which can influence an authority's culture, it does illustrate that for any effective change programme which aims to shift the authority from the left to the right side of the schedule, far more is needed than just structural or systems changes. Attitudinal change – such as the change from a blame culture to one which tolerates and learns from mistakes – is of at least equal importance.

A major factor omitted from the review is the importance of cultural leadership. All the gurus' studies of culture emphasise the critical importance of top managers acting as role models, and of the powerful influence of the single leader in shaping the character of an organisation. There is no great problem in the principle of local authority chief officers demonstrating the cultural qualities which are aimed for through their personal behaviour – though the practice may for some be rather more difficult. What may be more problematical is the matter of personal leadership. In a company, this can unquestionably be provided by the chairman or chief executive. But in a local authority, there are two forms of leadership – the political and the managerial. Which should be the major influence on the council's culture? The worst scenario is when the chief executive and the leader of the majority party (assuming the authority is not politically balanced) adopt or endorse markedly different styles. The political leader may, for example, be very informal, highly pragmatic and unconscious of status distinctions; the chief executive may project a much more formal and authoritative image and be a stickler for precision and precedent – or vice versa. Either way, it would be difficult for the authority to gain staff commitment to a clear-cut organisational style ('the way we do things around here') given the highly conflicting messages they will pick up from the two leaders' very different personal characteristics and behaviour. Another unhappy situation develops if the political leadership adopts the style which Charles Handy attributes to Zeus, becomes closely involved in day-to-day management, and browbeats the senior management into sullen submission. Local authorities cannot, or at least should not, be run as personal fiefdoms with the culture of the owner-managed small business. Ideally and practically, in this, as in other aspects of an authority's aims and activities, the political and managerial leadership should be in accord.

Footnotes:
1. *Building a Dynamic Corporation*, R Blake and J Mouton; Addison Wesley; 1969.
2. *Customer First*, D Walker; Gower; 1990.
3. *Encyclopedic dictionary of Organizational Behaviour*, N Nicholson (editor); Blackwell, 1995.
4. *Culture: A Critical review of Concepts and Definitions*, A Kroeber and C ; Vintage Books, 1952.
5. *Customer First*, D Walker.

Chapter 8

The flexible organisation

The general flexibility message

In prescriptions for organisational success, 'flexibility' is one of the most widely used words – even though the slant given to it varies between different management gurus. Three typical quotes are:

- "The organisations now emerging as successful will be, above all, flexible: they will need to be able to bring particular resources together quickly, on the basis of short term recognition of new requirements..."
  – Rosabeth Moss Kanter in *The Change Masters*.

- "Flexibility is the necessary watchword. Sound thinking and debate about the future, marked by the asking of novel questions, foster flexibility of thought and action".
  – Tom Peters in *Thriving on Chaos*.

- "World class excellence is continual improvement in serving the customer's four basic wants: ever-better quality, ever-lower costs, ever-increasing flexibility and ever-quicker response".
  – Richard Schonberger in *World Class Manufacturing*.

The basic idea is simple. Because of the rate and range of change in organisations' external environments, they need to be able to adapt and act quickly to meet new threats or exploit new opportunities. Old-style organisations, with their emphasis on detailed procedures, tall management hierarchies and centralised control, react too slowly to external change. Their prime characteristics are consistency, caution and effectiveness in maintaining the status quo. What is needed instead, in what Tom Peters describes as "an era of unprecedented uncertainty", are qualities of adaptability, innovation, rapidity of action – in a word, flexibility. Or in Rosabeth Moss Kanter's vivid metaphor, "the power of an elephant combined with the agility of a dancer". However, there are differences between the gurus in the emphasis given to different aspects of flexibility, some talking mainly of major changes to organisational structures, others of attitudinal change, and in recent times, a great deal of attention being directed towards flexibility in employment practices.

Enthusiasm for the concept, in general, needs to be tempered by the recognition that many of the gurus who have promoted it have been concerned with a specifically American problem – the declining competitiveness of major American business in world markets. The opening section of Moss Kanter's book, quoted above, is entitled *The Need for an American Corporate Renaissance*. Tom Peters sets out his remedies for rigidity against an analysis of an economic background which indicates that "our economic hegemony is at an end" – the 'our' being America. The widespread concern in the USA about the threat to American economic world domination of the rising tiger economies of the Pacific rim tended to generate an almost frenzied reaction among those who seemed to assume the USA had a divine right to be the world's numero uno. Some of the more extreme flexibility medicines, like Tom Peters' 'reinvent the organisation every day', consequently need to be taken with a small spoonful of salt.

That said, complacency about the capability of traditional organisations to cope successfully with change would be dangerously misplaced – a view which lies at the core of many of the writings of the internationally respected UK guru, Charles Handy. "We are", he says, "entering an age of unreason... a time when the only prediction that will hold true is that no prediction will hold true".[1] What Handy focuses on is not the plight of the large American corporation but – for the UK – the more immediately relevant impact of rapid technological change. In his bestseller, *The Age of Unreason*, he points particularly to information technology and bio-engineering as two forces which are reshaping the lives both of individuals and organisations. He explains that his arguments about the need for new, flexible forms of organisations are based on three assumptions:

- That the types of change we are now experiencing differ from previous experience in that change is now discontinuous. Change is proceeding by rapid jumps, not by a slow evolutionary process.
- That changes in the way work is organised will make the biggest difference to the way we all live.
- That discontinuous change requires "discontinuous, upside-down thinking to deal with it".

As with so many of the various gurus' ideas during the 1980s and 1990s, the concept of discontinuity had been highlighted many years earlier by Peter Drucker, in his 1969 book, *The Age of Discontinuity*. Drucker also demonstrated some upside-down thinking by suggesting the extensive 're-privatisation' of public services – using the that term rather than 'privatisation' to make the point that prior to the 19th century, the State was not involved in the provision and management of functions which later became identified with public ownership. Drucker's motivation did not appear to be political, but rather based on the view that government's role was to govern, not to get involved in organisational management.

Core and periphery

One of the most widespread ideas about the shape of flexible organisations is the 'core and periphery' model, which unlike many management theories, originated in the UK rather than the USA. In 1984, John Atkinson, a research fellow at the Institute of Manpower Studies (IMS), wrote one of the earliest articles in the management press to address the subject of flexibility and the first to describe this in core and periphery terms. Entitled *Manpower Strategies for Flexible Organisations*[2], the article suggested that companies were looking for three kinds of flexibility:

- Functional flexibility – primarily by developing the multi-skilled workforce, so that the same employees could quickly move from one type of work to another.
- Numerical flexibility – employment practices to enable the headcount to be rapidly increased or decreased in line with even short-term fluctuations in demand.
- Financial flexibility – so that pay (and pay costs) could be readily varied to reflect both changes in the pay market and in levels of performance.

The article went on to suggest that these flexibility objectives were being met by a new organisational model involving "the break-up of the orthodox hierarchical structure of the firm in such a way that radically different employment policies can be pursued for different group of workers". The flexible firm was consequently coming to consist of a relatively small core of full-time, permanent, multi-skilled career employees, surrounded by a periphery of other groups which provided the flexibility. The periphery consisted of:

- A first group of full-time employees enjoying (if that is the right word) "a lower level of job security and less access to career opportunities than the core employees". The jobs were the less skilled, and required little training because the job content was limited to a narrow range of tasks. This, together with the absence of career prospects, would result, so Atkinson suggested, in a relatively high level of labour turnover which would facilitate numerical flexibility.
- The second group provided even more flexibility in numbers. It consisted of staff on short term and temporary contracts, shift workers taken on to meet periodic work peaks and the like.
- On the outside rim of the periphery were agency staff, self-employed 'jobbers', sub-contractors and other forms of outsourcing.

Atkinson was describing what research by the IMS indicated was actually beginning to happen in British companies – not putting forward his personal views about the best way forward. So his analysis included some brutally frank assessments of the effects on employees of the core and periphery model:

> "The implications of these changes for employees is that an individual's pay, security and career opportunities will increasingly be secured at the expense of the employment conditions of others, often women, who will find themselves

permanently relegated to dead-end, insecure and low-paid jobs... At the core, job security, single status and performance-related pay systems contrast with the relatively poor conditions, insecurity and pay levels driven down by competition which are found among most peripheral groups... The numerical balance between these groups appears to be changing, with some managers anxious to push as many jobs as possible into the peripheral categories".

Developments in the decade following this article have shown just two weak points in Atkinson's otherwise very perceptive analysis. Job security in the core is probably less than he suggested; and the first group in the periphery has been almost wholly overtaken by the second. Creating numerical flexibility by treating some employees so badly that it resulted in high turnover was never going to be either sensible or effective – particularly during a recession in which people hung grimly on to whatever job they could. Hiring staff on temporary contracts and using freelances, homeworkers and other forms of outsourcing have been seen as far more effective – even if there are signs of some unease in some companies about the extent to which they have pushed jobs and work into the periphery. Doubts centre not so much on full-scale outsourcing but on an over-reliance on temporary staff whose primary concern is often (and very understandably) on where their next job will come from, rather than on their current work.

Charles Handy's types of flexible organisation
Many of the American gurus' exhortations to organisations to become more flexible are long on qualitative principles but short on practicalities. They tend to emphasise the importance of changes to managerial attitudes and the need to foster creativity and innovation, but say little about what all this means for organisational structure and the design of work. The major contribution to the flexibility debate of the British guru, Charles Handy, has been to suggest and describe three organisational models in fairly specific terms. He labels these:
- The shamrock organisation.
- The federal organisation.
- The Triple I organisation.

Linked to these three models of whole organisations is a concept of work – in terms of either individual jobs or teams. Handy labels this concept:
- The inverted doughnut.

Unlike Atkinson who simply analysed and described the trends identified by research, Handy's writings promote his own views about the need for flexibility and how this might be achieved.

The shamrock organisation: In *The Age of Unreason*, Handy explains that the shamrock is a three-leaved plant. It is not entirely clear why he selected this Irish emblem rather than the clover – except, perhaps, that the shamrock was used by St Patrick to symbolise the three-in-one of the Holy Trinity. Religion and botany aside, the point of Handy's shamrock concept is that the flexible organisation is composed of three different components – "three very different groups of people...

managed differently, paid differently, organised differently". The three leaves of the shamrock are:

- **The professional core:** the people who are essential to the organisation – mainly managers, technicians and the qualified professionals. They are hard to replace and are retained by high salaries and attractive fringe benefits. In return they are expected to be totally dedicated, work long hours and go wherever the organisation requires. Because they are expensive, they are few in number.
- **Contracted-out work:** all the work which can satisfactorily be done by other people and is consequently outsourced. Handy suggests that some organisations can take this as far as a 20/80 situation – 80% of the elements involved in the production of an organisation's goods or services being handled by contractors, self-employed individuals and other outside sources.
- **The flexible labour force:** employees on various forms of temporary, seasonal or variable contracts.

It is immediately evident that this concept has much in common with Atkinson's analysis, although there is no reference to the IMS research in Handy's book. It is also easier to picture the concept as a core surrounded by peripheral rings than as a three-leaved plant – particularly when, at the end of his chapter on the shamrock, Handy refers to the core as the hub of an organisational network. Leaves do not have hubs. However, in terms of guru literature, the shamrock organisation has had world-wide publicity whereas the idea of 'core and periphery' just seems to have evolved from its more modest origins.

Handy floated the idea that there may also be a fourth shamrock leaf, which if he had used the term 'clover-leaf organisation' could have been equated to the traditionally lucky four leaved clover. Metaphors aside, he suggested this additional element is "the growing practice of getting the customer to do the work". He instanced self-service in stores, hole-in-the wall cash dispensers, and automatic ticket machines. In 1997 he could add self-assessment of income tax.

In addition to describing his three (or four) leaves, Handy also discussed the management implications of the shamrock model:

- Staff in the core are not, thought Handy, people to be ordered around. They see themselves more as partners in the enterprise than as subordinates. They need to be given the freedom and authority to act and be rewarded handsomely for good results.
- Managerial control of the contractual fringe has to be exercised by specifying results, not by overseeing working methods. In selecting the functions for contracting-out, Handy thought it was wise to concentrate on 'boring work', but also not to attempt to get this done on the cheap. "Good work must receive good rewards or it will cease to be good work".
- Handy recognised the danger of the flexible labour force becoming "people of whom little is expected to whom little is given… Treated as casual labour such people behave casually". His remedy was to treat them as a valuable part of the organisation and provide training and benefits such as annual and sick leave.

Handy's ideas about the management of the flexible labour leaf – the seasonals, temporaries and the like – read rather thinly. No sooner does he commend treating them as a valuable resource than he qualifies this with a fairly pessimistic assessment:

> "The flexible labour force will never, however, have the commitment or ambition of the core. Decent pay and decent conditions is what they want. They... cannot be expected to rejoice in the organisation's triumphs... nor will they put themselves out for the love of it; more work in their culture deserves and demands more money... It is contract labour but the contract should be fair and must be honoured".

There is just a whiff of superiority and condescension about this – or perhaps a realistic acceptance of the fact that few, if any, organisations have fully solved the problem of gaining (or earning) genuine commitment from employees whose uncertain employment status gives little evidence of genuine reciprocal commitment by the employer.

Handy's final comment on the shamrock organisation is extremely important and highly relevant to public and private sector organisations which are attracted by the flexibility this model undoubtedly offers. He says the most difficult policy decision is what should be retained in the core. "The core is the critical hub of an organisational network. It is essential to get it right and manage it right".

The federal organisation: The federal organisation, in Handy's definition, is one in which the centre lets go and most activity, energy and power lies with its various, largely autonomous, units. Federalism is not the same as decentralisation. In the decentralised organisation, the centre delegates specific tasks and powers to its subordinate units but retains ultimate, overall direction or control. In the federal organisation, the centre's powers are given to it by the outlying units in what he describes as 'reverse delegation'. The flexibility comes from the freedom of each unit to do its own thing.

Not surprisingly, Handy found it difficult to produce actual business examples of this model, and fell back on using Switzerland as a parallel to what he had in mind. (In Switzerland, the limited powers of the federal government are derived largely from a consensus among the cantons as to what needs to be dealt with on a country-wide basis). Of Handy's three models, this has probably attracted the least attention.

The Triple I organisation: Handy often uses mock formulae to illustrate his ideas, and the 'Triple I organisation' is based on his $I^3 = AV$, where I stands for Intelligence, Information and Ideas and AV means Added Value. "New organisations", says Handy, "need new people to run them; people with new skills, new capacities and different career patterns". This is linked to the shamrock organisation, because the need for very bright people, supplied with leading edge information technology and generating very bright ideas is, in Handy's view, limited to the core. Unless the core operates on the Triple I principle, there will be no added value to pay for the support services. In his description of this model,

Handy emphasises the need for a new style of management. It is not a description which involves any very specific systems or structure – except to the extent that the hierarchy will be flat and that significant use will be made of outsourcing and the flexible fringe of non-core employees. The key to the effective Triple I approach, in Handy's view, is the acceptance by top management that "intelligent people cannot be commanded", and "intelligent people prefer to agree than obey". So the management of Triple I organisations has to be by persuasion, involvement and consent. One implication for the way work is done is that individuals will have a large degree of discretion in the methods they use – provided only that they produce results.

This organisational model, when linked to the shamrock (or core-and-periphery) has undoubtedly attracted attention from many major companies. Place a small core of highly intelligent and proactive people at the centre, pay them extremely well on the basis of results, give them freedom to innovate – these are characteristics which some companies see as the key to achieving the commercial imagination and flexibility needed to open new markets, exploit opportunities and combat business threats. The downside, however, is a possible lack of effective control which in extreme cases can lead to disasters as at Barings and Morgan Grenfell.

The inverted doughnut: Handy's yen for colourful metaphors does not always provide the immediate insight into his ideas which he probably intends. The 'inverted doughnut' (which his book irritatingly insists on spelling as do'nut) comes into this category and he has to explain this curious object before using it to illustrate a valuable concept about the nature of individual jobs and group tasks. The doughnut (or bagel) is the American version with a hole in the middle. But in the inverted doughnut, the middle is filled in and the hole is on the outside.

Applying the principle of this curious confection to jobs results in the idea that a job has a core of essential responsibilities or tasks, but that these do not constitute the totality of what is involved in doing the job well. Effective individuals take the initiative in making improvements, exploring new ways of doing things, going beyond the formal requirements of their roles. In doing so, they are, in Handy's terms, moving into the empty space of the inverted doughnut. No-one can tell them precisely what these extra activities must be – if they could be specified they would be part of the core.

Handy accepts that, in his words, "Some do'nuts are all core and no space". He instances the bus driver who must adhere to a set route and timetable, and suggests that the majority of the relatively straightforward jobs in the flexible labour leaf of the shamrock would be mostly core. But for individuals and groups in the intelligent core of the Triple I organisation, and for the units in a federal organisation, small cores and large surrounding spaces are needed. In putting forward this view, Handy recognises that it poses a challenge to traditional concepts of management. Many managers feel they should specify what has to be done and how it should be done, and feel most comfortable when everything is clearly defined. The new manager must learn to let go, to act as coach and counsellor rather than director or inspector, and accept that mistakes will occur at times within the undefined spaces of the organisation's doughnuts.

Like the Triple I concept, there has been widespread intellectual acceptance of the inverted doughnut concept (even if the metaphor has become confused with the core and periphery model). Putting it into practice has not generally proved so easy. This is partly for attitudinal reasons, with many managers at all levels reluctant to relinquish close control; but partly, too, because of genuinely difficult issues relating to the need to control expenditure and maintain corporate standards of probity, customer responsiveness and employee management.

Flexibility and the local authority

While councils may not need quite the same degree of flexibility as commercial enterprises, fluctuations in government grants, changes in legislation and in local economic and social circumstances, are all being experienced more frequently and to a greater degree than in the past. Authorities need to be able to move quickly, redeploy financial and staff resources to meet new circumstances and cope with the expansion and contraction of services without the costs of carrying surplus staff or experiencing staff shortages. The demand for value for money also requires an ability to change the source of support functions or service delivery to obtain the best mix of quality and cost. All this points to the advantages of building more flexibility into local authorities structures and practices than the old-style, centralised and rule-bound council could possibly achieve. The two most significant ideas about organisational flexibility in the gurus' literature for local authorities are consequently:

- The concept of the organisational core.
- Flexible employment practices.

The organisational core: It is probably the case that the recent wave of activity among authorities in deciding the function and constituent elements of their cores has been triggered more by white collar CCT than by any great enthusiasm for applying new management concepts. For many councils, defining the activities to be placed in the proportion of work exempt from CCT has begun as a defensive reaction, not a constructive approach to clarifying and strengthening their primary purpose. However, it has soon become clear that the process of defining the purpose and nature of the core is a very valuable exercise, regardless of CCT. It has encouraged authorities to debate their fundamental role and in particular to question the conventional assumption that this is simply the direct delivery of a specific range of services. A discussion paper published by the Local Government Training Board in 1990[4] suggested that a council's core function was "the provision of an institution whereby local communities can have a say in the management of their own affairs". The paper went on to develop this concept, saying: "To an increasing extent, if the local authority is to maintain a position of influence and achievement it needs to act as a facilitator of action, a co-ordinator of other institutions' contribution to the local good and as a pressure group – not just a service provider".

Applying these ideas to the structure of the centre (or core) of an authority results in a very different configuration from the traditional departmental grouping of large, administratively biased finance, legal, personnel and estates functions. To quote again from the LGTB paper:

"The emphasis switches towards small numbers of people who work across conventional professional boundaries and include experts in such areas as market research, the voluntary sector and economic development. Moreover, central staffing benefits from more fluid configurations than the rigidity of conventional organisation charts permits. Much of the work is of a project nature and can be handled by teams drawn for temporary periods from operational services, guided by a small number of central facilitators".

One major implication is the judicious use of voluntary outsourcing, partly as a means of gaining more flexibility in the choice of service provider, partly to enable the authority to focus more clearly on its core role and functions.

There are, of course, much wider reasons for defining this core role than just the achievement of more organisational flexibility. It is an element in the debate about the role of councils as units of local **government,** as distinct from acting as administrative agents of central government in the organisation of nationally prescribed services. In the flexibility context, however, the small, multi-functional core, concentrating on strategic issues and on the development of contacts and partnerships with a wide range of external organisations, is an essential element in achieving the type of responsiveness and adaptability in the public sector which parallels the characteristics the gurus consider is vital for survival in the commercial world.

Flexible employment practices: The shamrock and core and periphery models both suggest the need for a range of employment practices which are far less rigid than conventional, full-time, permanent employment. Growth in the use by local authorities of part-time and temporary staff, fixed term contracts and the like, are indications of an acceptance of the need for more flexibility – though in some cases the motivation has probably been more to reduce costs than to improve responsiveness. The benefits of flexibility have figured in several Audit Commission reports – most directly in recommendations flowing from the People, Pay and Performance review. In addition to general points about the desirability of flatter management hierarchies, the Commission's manual[5] goes into some detail about workforce flexibility. It provides a schedule of flexible employment practices which together with ideas drawn from other sources such as the Society of Chief Personnel Officers can be categorised under four headings:

- Flexibility in work and job design.
- Flexibility in staff deployment.
- Flexibility in working time.
- Flexibility in employee resourcing.

There are two main ways in which flexibility can be built into the way work is organised:

- Jobs can be broadened to include a wider range of responsibilities and activities. Fluctuations or changes in particular work elements can then be more readily absorbed within the multi-functional jobs, instead of some employees in narrowly defined jobs becoming under- or over-loaded.
- Staff can be developed by formal training and planned work experience to become multi-skilled and thus have the capability of doing more than one job. Changes in work requirements can then be met by rapid redeployment, instead of staff with a narrow range of skills becoming redundant and new skills having to be acquired through recruitment.

The advantages of multi-skilling cannot be fully achieved if an authority retains traditionally rigid and time-consuming systems of establishment control. At the extreme, these systems have required even the most minor of staffing changes (such as the transfer of one clerical post from one section to another) to be referred to committee for members' approval. The flexible authority will devolve authority to form and reform staff configurations to appropriate levels of management. With overall budgetary limits, unit managers will have freedom to deploy their staff as they wish – for example, to reduce the proportion of higher paid professional staff by employing more technicians, or to establish and disband sections or teams as changes in circumstances require.

There are several ways of introducing more flexibility into working time, so that seasonal or week to week variations in workloads can be dealt with other than by expensive overtime or carrying under-utilised staff:

- Part-time employment in evening or weekend shifts on plain time rates to cover regular peaks of demand.
- Part-time employment with variable weekly hours to cope with work which fluctuates between weeks. The contracts specify that weekly hours will average a certain amount (say 20) over the year but may vary between certain limits (say 12 to 25) in any one week.
- Annual hours contracts for full-time staff. Employees contract to work a total number of hours annually (equivalent to normal, full-time employment), are paid a standard weekly or monthly wage based on these hours, but if necessary work for varying periods on a daily or weekly basis to cope with fluctuations in workload.
- Seasonal variations, particularly for work outdoors such as grounds maintenance, with a short working week in the winter and a longer week (without overtime pay) in the summer.
- Home-based working, with pay based on the amount of work done rather than on the time taken to do it.

Flexibility in employee resourcing can involve a variety of different types of employment contract, including:

- Term-time only employment in schools and school-related jobs in education

departments, or seasonal employment in other services subject to significant seasonal fluctuations.
- Fixed term contracts for which their non-renewal does not legally amount to redundancy or unfair dismissal. (A waiver clause to this effect is needed in the contract).
- Contracts for performance – a legal term describing contracts which specify that employment will last until a specific task or project has been completed, or until specified circumstances occur. The date of the end time need not be known, provided the contract can clearly define the circumstances which will bring employment to an end. This is a more flexible arrangement than the fixed term contract.
- Standby or supply employment – a long-standing system for teachers, but one which might have wider application for other work for which some people would be interested in being on a register to be called on for temporary spells of employment.

Temporary employment is not listed because employment law does not recognise this as a special category. A so-called temporary employee acquires the same employment rights as a permanent employee (i.e. someone on an open-ended contract) if they are employed continuously for the varying periods which give statutory access to these rights. In addition, the practice of some private sector employees of describing some employees as temporary and dismissing them just before they acquire unfair dismissal rights is not one which any self-respecting local authority would wish to emulate.

It has been noted earlier in this chapter that while promoting the concept of employee flexibility, the gurus are uneasy about the effect on commitment and motivation of practices which involve a large degree of job insecurity or only short-term employment. The implication for local authorities is to place more emphasis on job design, deployment and working time than on those aspects of employee resourcing in which uncertainty about the duration of employment is the primary source of flexibility. Outsourcing, while stressful for employees at the time functions are contracted out, may also have the effect of reducing uncertainty and insecurity for the core and contract management staff who remain, as well as being itself one means of enhancing organisational flexibility.

Footnotes:
1. *The Age of Uncertainty* (2nd edition 1991), Charles Handy, Arrow Business Books 1995.
2. *Manpower Strategies for Flexible Organisations*, John Atkinson, *Personnel Management*, August 1984.
3. *The Age of Uncertainty*, Charles Handy.
4. *Organisational Value from the Centre*, Alan Fowler, LGTB, 1990.
5. *People Pay and Performance: Management Handbook*, Audit Commission, 1995.

Chapter 9

The learning organisation

The development of the concept

The wide international interest in the concept of the learning organisation has been largely a follow on from the ideas about organisational excellence which were discussed in chapter 3. A number of the companies which met the criteria Peters and Waterman expounded in *In Search of Excellence* later foundered, and the obvious question was why. Was it because ISOE got it all wrong or were other factors involved which that book failed to address? The conclusion of most management gurus was that companies such as IBM and People Express got into such deep doodoo because they failed to respond to new circumstances. They displayed characteristics of excellence and outstanding success in the commercial environment at the time Peters and Waterman were writing, but did not react effectively when the environment changed. In brief, they had not learned to adapt.

This focused attention on the idea that not just managers as individuals, but organisations as corporate entities, could and should develop learning capabilities. The whole idea was propelled into the international managerial arena in 1990 by a best-selling book by Peter Senge, a director at the Sloan School of Management – part of the world famous Massachusetts Institute of Technology. This book, *The Fifth Discipline*, was sub-titled *The Art and Practice of the Learning Organization*[1] and is often credited with being the first exposition of the concept. In reality, as Senge himself says, many of the ideas involved were drawn from earlier sources, while in the UK, even the term itself had been pre-empted in 1987 in a book by Bob Garratt, a management consultant and academic, entitled *The Learning Organisation*. One of Garratt's messages to top managers was to adopt a 'hands off, brains on' approach and not be diverted from strategic thinking and visioning by short term firefighting.

In articles in the academic and management press, Garratt has also argued that many of the key ideas about organisational learning were evolved in the UK in the 1960s and 1970s by Reg Revans, a one time local government officer with Essex County Council and later academic. His book *Action Learning*, published in 1979, argued that an essential feature of the learning process in any type of organisation was the sharing of problems between the organisation's members. Or as he put it: "Groups of comrades in adversity, striving to learn with and from each other as they confess failures and expand on victories".[2] Revan's ideas about learning in groups, which are fully consistent with current thinking about the learning organisation, made very little impact at the time within the UK. Oddly, he was far more successful as a consultant in gaining support for action learning in India, Egypt and Nigeria.

Peter Senge and the Fifth Discipline

It is undoubtedly true that many of Senge's ideas can be traced back to the work of earlier gurus such as Chris Argyris on 'double-loop learning' (explained later in this chapter) and other writers on learning theory, systems theory and the management of change. Senge himself quotes upwards of 100 sources for his ideas, though these omit Garratt, and even a chapter on team learning makes no reference to Revans, for whom learning in teams formed the basis of effective organisational development. One of the irritating features of some American gurus' writings is the way they overlook or ignore the works of British management thinkers and practitioners.

However, that does not alter the fact that *The Fifth Discipline* put the learning organisation firmly alongside empowerment, re-engineering and total quality as one of the managerial buzzwords which have become so widely used as almost to lose any defined meaning. Senge argues that a true learning organisation must integrate five so-called 'component technologies', or disciplines:

- **Systems thinking:** the ability to see the linkages and reciprocal influences of all the different parts and processes of the organisation's activities and its relationship with the outside world. The concept has some similarity with the emphasis on whole processes, rather than individual tasks, in business process re-engineering.
- **Personal mastery:** the organisation's encouragement of its people to commit themselves to lifelong learning and personal development – the link between individual and corporate learning. By mastery, Senge means a high level of proficiency, not domination.
- **Mental models:** understanding, and if necessary changing, the often unconscious assumptions or generalisations which influence people's behaviour or perceptions of priorities. One example might be the use of 7-S as a mental map to guide an organisation's management of change.
- **Building shared vision:** developing and promoting what Senge calls 'pictures of the future' which provide the inspiration for people to learn and excel.
- **Team learning:** developing the potential for the effectiveness of a team to be more than the sum of its parts. Senge says: "Team learning is vital because teams, not individuals, are the fundamental learning unit in modern organisations... Unless teams can learn, the organisation cannot learn".

Somewhat confusingly, the 'fifth discipline' of the book's title is the first in Senge's list – systems thinking. "It is", says Senge, "the discipline that integrates the disciplines, turning them into a coherent body of theory and practice". For example, vision without systems thinking may well result in splendid pictures of the future which are unattainable because the means of achievement have not been thought through. Systems thinking, says Senge:

> "makes understandable the subtlest aspect of the learning organisation – the new way individuals perceive themselves and their world. At the heart of a learning organisation is a shift of mind – from seeing ourselves as separate from the world to connected to the world; from seeing problems as caused by someone or something 'out there' to seeing how our own actions create the problems we experience".

And in his basic definition of the learning organisation, Senge describes it as an organisation that is "continually expanding its capacity to create its future".

All of which is interesting intellectually but not, perhaps, of much immediate use to busy chief executives who want to know what practical action they should take to develop their organisations' learning capabilities. A major problem with Senge's book is that it is very long on descriptions of desirable outcomes and very short on the steps needed to achieve them – other than to emphasise in a variety of different ways that the key to effective learning is to change the way people think. Even the chapter on 'personal mastery' – the nearest the book comes to addressing the practicalities of learning – is about attitudes and vision, not how people learn in real terms or what action an organisation should take to encourage individual development.

The chapter begins by acknowledging that "organisations learn only through individuals who learn… From their quest for continual learning comes the spirit of the learning organisation". Senge's description of the components of this personal learning process within an organisational environment can be summarised as:

- Individuals continually clarify what is important to them.
- Individuals continually learn to see current reality more clearly.
- The organisation is unequivocally committed to encouraging personal development and success, and values this as highly as financial success.
- The organisation links its support for individual development to a shared vision and shared mental models.
- Personal mastery involves the discipline of focusing on personal visions.
- The gap between current reality and the personal vision should be seen as a source of creative tension – not as a cause for anxiety or depression.
- Commitment to the truth and the avoidance of self-deception.
- Integrating intuition and reason – recognising that intuitive ideas often stem from a better understanding of whole systems than a rational analysis may provide.
- Recognising connections between actions and outcomes – developing the feedback learning loop.
- Developing understanding and empathy with other people and their situations and visions.

- For top management: acting as role models by continually showing a commitment to personal learning.

Given the abstract and philosophical nature of most of *The Fifth Discipline*, it may seem surprising that the book achieved best-seller status and has had so strong an influence on organisational theory. It is evident, however, that a concept which draws on sources as wide-ranging as Albert Einstein, Picasso, Leo Tolstoy, various Eastern philosophers and several American and Japanese business leaders does have appeal to some managers. But it is better read as a source of personal inspiration than as any type of organisational learning manual.

Ideas about learning from other gurus

In 1978, the American organisational psychologist and consultant Chris Argyris published *Organizational Learning*, a book which Peter Senge acknowledged as a significant source of ideas about the learning organisation – unsurprisingly when one considers the title. Criticised by fellow guru Peter Drucker for being too idealistic, the book emphasised the extent to which employees' innate potential was often stifled by managerial defensiveness caused by a fear of losing control. Dealing specifically with the learning process, Argyris's main link with Senge's ideas was his exposition of single and double loop learning – a concept which Senge applied throughout *The Fifth Discipline*.

Single loop learning occurs when there is a match between an organisation's intentions and what actually happens – or when a mis-match occurs which is quickly recognised and corrected without questioning underlying assumptions. Double loop learning occurs when assumptions about the cause of errors are questioned and the underlying reasons for mis-matches between intention and outcome are dealt with. Put another way, single loop learning involves addressing the immediate and obvious details of a problem and taking obvious but narrowly focused action. Double loop learning involves developing an understanding of the broad context within which the problem occurred and correcting the cause rather than simply dealing with the symptoms. The idea is that single loop learning may do little more than reinforce existing perceptions and attitudes, while double loop learning requires a mind open to new ideas. This links directly with Senge's fifth and key discipline – systems thinking. Both gurus see organisational learning as involving an ability and willingness to examine and question whole systems or processes and to see the links between what may superficially seem to be unconnected functions or influences.

A somewhat more operational approach to the learning organisation was summarised in an article in *People Management* in 1995[3] by the British co-author of *The Learning Company*, John Burgoyne. His description of organisational learning processes included:

- A learning approach to strategy.
- Participative policy making; involving people throughout the organisation.
- 'Informating' – internal openness and dialogue through the application of information technology.

- Accounting and control which provides feedback that can be learnt from.
- Systems of reward which provide incentives for learning and the sharing of lessons learnt.
- Simple organisational structures which facilitate learning and allow the consequences of learning to be applied.
- 'Boundary workers acting as environmental scanners' – staff who are in close touch with the organisation's external environment.
- Learning from and with other organisations through benchmarking and other comparative studies.
- A culture that encourages and supports learning from experience and self-development by individuals.

Although this does not provide a detailed operational blueprint, it does suggest some aspects – such as benchmarking and environmental monitoring – which are rather more specific than some other gurus' advice which in essence amounts to a plea for managers to stop being defensive and start being more open to new experiences and ideas.

Ultimately, the learning organisation relies on managers being good learners and in this context, the work of another UK management academic and consultant, Alan Mumford, is highly relevant. He argues that the most powerful source of managers' personal development is learning by and from experience, rather than through formal management education and training. He accepts that formal training has a role to play, but points to research which indicates that experiences such as taking responsibility for a difficult project or working in a multi-disciplinary team can be far more influential on a manager's development. In one of his several books on this subject, *Developing Top Managers*,[4] in which he also draws on the work of his consultancy colleague, Peter Honey, he sets this approach to individual learning in an organisational context:

> "The vital point about organisational learning is that learning for managers is a social process and is therefore responsive to group processes and to an overall organisational climate… An organisation encourages learning if:
> — it encourages managers to identify their open learning needs and sets challenging learning goals;
> — it encourages managers to experiment;
> — it provides opportunities for learning both on and off the job;
> — it gives on the spot feedback;
> — it allows time for managers to plan, review and conclude learning activities;
> — it tolerates some mistakes provided managers try to learn from them".

One of Mumford's points is that if learning from experience is so powerful, organisations should plan to make effective use of it. This involves looking for learning opportunities, discussing learning as well as task objectives when work projects are allocated, and giving and discussing feedback about what has been learned when the task has been completed. Mumford has also promoted the concept of 'unlearning' – the need for managers and organisations to discard ideas and solutions which may once have been appropriate but are now out-dated.

Local authorities as learning organisations

What can local authorities apply from the wide range of often rather abstract ideas which constitute the gurus' descriptions of the learning organisation? Two of the more general principles are of very direct relevance to the nature and role of the local authority:

- The need to become highly responsive to the external environment – to learn about and from the institutions and people with whom the authority needs to interact.
- The need to adopt systems thinking – looking at whole processes and the links and influences between internal units and functions.

Local authorities, by virtue of their unique role as the democratically elected voice of their communities, need to be acutely aware of what is going on locally. They need to know about other organisations' activities which may affect the interests of local people. They need to be in close touch with the concerns and aspirations of their citizens and of the many special interest groups which exist in every location across the country. In short, they need to learn to look at themselves from the outside – to see themselves from the perspective of the people and institutions they should serve or influence. This implies a major cultural change for the more traditional council and its managers who, probably unconsciously, have been more concerned with internal administrative efficiency and the defence of internal power structures than with any great enthusiasm for learning from the complicated world outside.

Probably all authorities if asked, would now support the concept of the responsive, adaptable and learning council. But achieving this requires much more than good intentions or the circulation of *The Fifth Discipline* around the management team. Authorities which are determined to break out of the conventional bureaucratic (or 'we know best') mould have introduced new structures and systems to provide a framework for action. Examples of such measures include:

- The monitoring of service-user satisfaction by methods such as response/comment cards, complaints procedures and periodic opinion surveys.
- The use of focus groups or panels of citizens to help identify issues of interest or concern, and to sound out reaction to possible service changes.
- Setting up users' consultative panels for specific services, such as sports and arts centres; or co-opting users' representatives onto management committees.
- Holding regular meetings with representatives of special interest groups to discuss needs and opportunities.
- Forming consultative committees of invited or elected representatives of community, business and interest groups to act as advisers to the relevant formal committees.
- Ensuring the committee and management structures can deal effectively with

subjects such as green issues, vandalism and economic development, which are of major local concern but which cross conventional service boundaries.
- Designating some senior staff to act specifically as 'boundary workers' – getting out and around in the local community to build up a network of external relationships.

This is not an exhaustive list, but it illustrates the point that the authority which wishes to learn about, and learn from, its outside world, needs to take practical action to provide structures and mechanisms for real, practical progress to be made.

This externally-oriented approach needs to be mirrored internally, to promote mutual understanding and learning within the organisational structure and to develop holistic systems thinking. Practical measures which can be seen in a growing number of authorities include:
- Re-grouping previously separate and narrowly defined functions into broader-based operations. One example from a large county is the formation of an internal management consultancy unit which combines previously separate management services, IT, and value-for-money audit staff.
- Establishing multi-disciplinary team-working, instead of each discipline having its own professional structure. For example, one authority's property management department has area-based teams which each include architects, quantity surveyors, environmental engineers and clerks of works – who were all once in separate sections.
- The widespread use of inter-departmental project teams to progress specific, time-limited initiatives.
- Involving junior or front-line staff in status-free project teams or in other forms of discussion about service quality, plans and progress.
- The use of brainstorming sessions to generate ideas for new ways of working and to improve quality.
- The routine use of de-briefing and discussion meetings to review particular events – including failures or mistakes – to ensure everything possible is learned for future application.

Initiatives of all these kinds need also to be linked with another important theme on which all the learning organisation gurus agree – the creating of a working environment and the use of developmental systems which encourage and support individual learning. One of the features of the Audit Commission's 1995 study of performance management was that the most effective employee appraisal systems are those which combine work-based targets with personal development objectives. In a similar way, measures designed to open up the authority as a whole to learning more effectively from external and internal experience are unlikely to be fully effective unless managers (and staff at large) display a similar open approach to identifying and satisfying their own learning needs.

Within limits, this can be aided by a fairly conventional approach to training, particularly if this includes in-house training courses to explain and reinforce relevant aspects of the authority's approach, such as customer care. But as Alan

Mumford points out, formal off-the-job training accounts for only a relatively small part of any manager's real learning experience. There is consequently a value in positive action to exploit the learning opportunities which can be provided by:

- The experience of working in a multi-disciplinary project team and thereby learning about other functions. Staff can be selected for team membership with their learning objectives in mind, as well as the task objectives.
- Secondments of staff to work for periods in other departments, or externally. Some authorities arrange secondments to companies such as Marks & Spencer or organisations in the voluntary sector or the Civil Service.
- Allocating experienced staff to act as mentors to their less experienced colleagues.
- Ensuring that learning needs and opportunities are discussed within the context of staff appraisal systems.

The authority can also provide support to employees' individual learning initiatives by such means as:

- Setting up a learning resource centre, stocked with self-teaching packages such as training videos, inter-active CDs, computerised training programmes, training material from the Local Government Management Board and relevant books and professional journals. The centre can be open for any employee to use during lunch breaks and before and after work.
- Helping employees to prepare personal reading or other study programmes, and providing or subsidising the material involved.
- Sponsoring personal distance-learning studies, such as the courses available from the Open Business School.
- Assisting employees who are members of relevant professional institutes obtain the experience they may need to meet their institutes' requirements for 'continuing professional development'. (Most institutes now require evidence of positive action to keep up-to-date as an ongoing criterion for continued membership).

These are all practical measures which an authority can take at the corporate and individual level to develop the concept and reality of the learning organisation. To be fully effective, one other element is needed – the full commitment of elected members and top management to a culture which encourages the exploration of new ideas, a receptiveness to external influences, and a willingness to learn from one's own mistakes and from the views and experience of others. A genuine climate of lifetime learning – organisational and individual – cannot be achieved solely by changing structures and systems.

Footnotes:
1. *The Fifth Discipline*, Peter Senge; Century Business, 1990.
2. *The Learning Organization*, Bob Garratt; Fontana Collins, 1987.
3. *Feeding Minds to Grow the Business*, John Burgoyne; *People Management* 21st September, 1995.
4. *Management Development*, Alan Mumford; IPM, 1989.

Chapter 10

Total quality management (TQM)

How the concept developed

Current quality management theories were evolved within the context of Japanese and American manufacturing industry. In brief, two consultants from the States – W Edwards Deming and Joseph Juran – worked in the 1950s on the regeneration of Japanese industry after its devastation in the Second World War. They were concerned particularly to overcome the pre-war reputation of Japanese goods as cheap and shoddy, and consequently made quality the principle emphasis of their advice to Japan's industrial leaders. In the States, little attention was paid to their views until the early 1980s, when panic set in about the diminishing competitiveness of American industry in the face of increasingly successful Japanese exports. Phillip Crosby had attracted considerable interest (though little activity) in the subject with his 1979 book, *Quality is Free*, but the trigger for the quality movement in the USA was a 1980 television programme, *If Japan Can, Why Can't We?*

In the resultant upsurge of interest in quality, Deming and Juran were joined by several other gurus in the USA, notably Armand Feigenbaum. An emphasis on delivering quality to the customer has since become an element of almost every management guru's analysis of the characteristics of the successful enterprise. In the main, UK management writers and consultants have done little more than add supportive commentaries to the theories of their American counterparts, although one UK author, Ron Collard, has written a book – *Total Quality: success through people*[1] – which focuses specifically on the human resource aspects of the subject.

One of the reasons why it took some 20 years for Deming and Juran's ideas to be picked up in the West may have been that neither wrote a book on the subject until the 1980s. Juran had produced a quality control handbook in 1951 but this was not the type of publication which takes off as a management best-seller. Both consultants wrote articles and lectured extensively on quality, but the absence of a widely publicised and hard-hitting text, together with complacency about the superiority of American industry, contributed to the Japanese gaining a head start in the quality stakes. Even after the message of the 1980 television programme had hit the headlines in the USA, there was considerable delay before very much more was published. Deming's somewhat technical *Quality, Productivity and Competitive Position* came out in 1982 but it was not until his more popular book, *Out of the Crisis*, was published in 1986, that many managers really grasped the full significance of his quality message. Juran's only book, *Juran on Planning for Quality*, was published even later in 1988. As authors, neither Deming nor Juran are as readable as Tom Peters, Rosabeth Moss Kanter or Charles Handy, and some of the clearest accounts of their ideas have been written by other people, notably Mary Walton's *The Deming Management Method.*[2]

Phillip Crosby's second and best-selling book *Quality Without Tears*, published in 1984,[3] helped plug the gap in the quality literature in the mid 80s, together with Armand Fiegenbaum's *Total Quality Control.*[4] From 1990 onwards, the number of books and articles on various aspects of quality has escalated and no one guru stands out as the current quality leader. Deming, who died in 1993 (at the age of 93), will probably always be thought of as the father of quality management – not least because of the extent to which he is revered in Japan and his memory kept alive there by the highly prestigious annual Deming Prize awards.

In the UK, although the high profile quality movement did not take off until the mid to late 1980s, the British Standards Institute had quietly pre-empted at least some aspects of this in 1979 with the launch of the quality standard, BS 5750. No-one took very much notice at the time, and little use was made of the standard until the whole quality issue blew up in the late 1980s. Since then, BS 5750 has become the basis for the later development of the international ISO 9000 standards, while a requirement for quality certification, particularly in public sector tendering, has become a common practice. In the public sector, too, the government's Charter Mark initiative has provided institutionalised encouragement and recognition of quality in the sense of customer responsiveness.

In parallel to TQM, and with many similarities, has been the development of value management – variously termed value analysis and value engineering. VM is described later in this chapter.

Curiously, the phrase 'total quality management', widely used in its acronymic form, TQM, cannot be attributed to any one guru. The various labels given to the subject by the quality gurus include:

- Deming – 'management for quality'.
- Juran – 'company-wide quality management'.
- Feigenbaum – 'total quality control'.
- Crosby – 'right first time' and 'zero defects'.

The label TQM has emerged as commentators on the works of the principal gurus have attempted to achieve a synthesis of all the ideas involved. A dictionary definition is:

"Total quality management (TQM) is a management philosophy and business strategy intended to embed quality improvement practices deeply into the fabric of the organization. It is also a social movement which has become partly institutionalised in many countries".[5]

Although this global approach to TQM is helpful because it emphasises the strategic philosophy involved (i.e. strategy before systems, in a 7-S context), a brief outline of the main differences between the gurus provides a wider choice of approaches when attempting to adapt TQM ideas to the world of the public services.

The Deming philosophy

Deming was a physicist and statistician by profession and his original approach to quality was strongly influenced by the development in the 1920s and 1930s of techniques such as statistical process control and the application of statistical analysis to quality control in the manufacturing industry. At the heart of these techniques and of Deming's later work was the idea that quality improves as variability in production is reduced. Consequently, and despite the greater publicity which has been given to the philosophical and humanist aspects of his quality message, Deming's work at the practical or factory level included the use of sophisticated statistical analysis to provide the data needed for effective quality information and control.

What he realised, however, was that these statistical tools would only be used effectively within an organisational culture which promoted quality as a core value. His ideas gradually evolved into a 14 point philosophy which has been variously described by different commentators and has changed several times, but can be summarised as:

1. Work constantly towards improving the quality of the organisation's products – goods or services.
2. Adopt 'kaizen' – the Japanese philosophy of continual incremental product improvement.
3. Do not rely on quality inspection – build quality into the basic design and manufacture of the product.
4. Abandon the practice of selecting tenders on a lowest price basis: work with suppliers to ensure the fitness for purpose and quality of outsourced goods and services.
5. Constantly decrease costs by constantly improving quality and productivity.
6. Institute on the job training for everybody – including managers.
7. See supervision and management in terms of leadership and support – helping people to improve their performance.
8. Do not use fear as a method of managing people: develop effective two-way communication: motivate and enthuse.
9. Break down traditional barriers between functions and occupations: use multi-functional teams.
10. Do not attempt to get results from the workforce by exhortations and slogans: they only generate cynicism and resentment.
11. Do not set statistical quotas or targets: substitute supportive supervision, training, the right equipment and the use of best methods.
12. Remove practices such as performance pay and management by objectives which undermine pride in work.

13. Encourage and support self-development throughout the workforce to keep pace with the need for new knowledge and skills.
14. Ensure and demonstrate top management's commitment to quality and continuous improvement.

Deeming said his 14 point plan was neither a menu from which individual items could be selected nor a detailed blueprint. It was a philosophy or culture – the characteristics of an organisation which sets customer satisfaction as its principal aim. The unusual mixture of detailed statistical method and broad philosophy in Deming's concept has created difficulties. How, for example, can his rubbishing of quantified targets and objectives be reconciled with his use of numeric data for quality analysis and control? On balance, it is the philosophical and cultural aspects of his work which have received most acclaim in the West – although the Japanese appear to have no difficulty in applying both the detail and generality of his ideas.

Juran's approach

Juran, although by training an engineer, was critical of the statistical emphasis in Deming's work, while respecting and largely agreeing with the cultural elements. Juran's approach is based on a 'quality trilogy' of:

- Quality planning, which includes incorporating quality targets in business plans.
- Quality management, including error reduction and a methodology for identifying and controlling the costs of a quality programme.
- Quality improvement, which is very much in line with much of Deming's approach.

He adopted a more radical stance than Deming by advocating the need for revolutionary organisational or cultural change rather than incremental or project-by-project improvement. If you are up to your waist in alligators, said Juran, the project approach would require you to kill the alligators one by one. Better, therefore, to drain the swamp.

He agreed with Deming that the responsibility for achieving or maintaining a quality-oriented organisation lies squarely with management, claiming that at least 80% of quality problems are directly attributable to factors which managers can control. He is also in accord with Deming in his message that a commitment to quality must permeate the whole organisation, across all functions, and from top to bottom.

Crosby and Feigenbaum

For many managers, the main appeal of Phillip Crosby's approach is his claim that effective quality programmes produce financial savings. Unlike the other quality gurus, Crosby's background is in industrial management, where he was vice-president of ITT before setting up his own quality consultancy. Savings, he claims – and quotes figures to prove it – accrue from cutting out the cost of defects and remedial work. He has criticised other quality professionals for failing to pay sufficient attention to the financial aspects of the subject and for not commending the practice of setting cost-reduction targets. In this, he has been supported by another consultant, Richard Schonberger, who is generally credited with introducing 'just in time' manufacturing systems to American industry. Schonberger and Crosby both emphasise that customers do not simply want good quality goods and services – they also want lower prices.

However, Crosby's approach has not been limited to a cost/benefit analysis. He has suggested 'Four Absolutes' for effective quality management:

- The recognition that quality is not absolute, or in his words, 'goodness'. It is conformity with requirements. This is an important concept, because it helps to avoid the notion that everything must be done to Rolls Royce standards. If the customer specifies something cheap and cheerful – a Mini rather than a Roller – the quality organisation meets that requirement.
- The way to produce quality is through a system which prevents defects, not by post-production inspection or appraisal. The aim is 'Right First Time'.
- 'Close enough' to requirements is not good enough – the target must be 'Zero Defects'.
- Quality is best measured by assessing the cost of failing to meet customers' requirements.

When talking of customers, Crosby does not mean only the final consumers or end users. He, with Schonberger, sees most business processes as having chains of customers between the supplier of raw materials and the user of the final product. Included in this chain are the organisation's internal units – the in-house purchasers and providers, to use current market jargon.

Feigenbaum, who was once the head of quality control at GEC, places a similar emphasis to Crosby on calculating – and then cutting – the costs of poor quality. He calculated that some 15% to 40% of capacity in some American service companies was engaged in resolving failures of various kinds and concluded this was a principal reason for their very poor record of productivity achievement. In the UK, the Department of Trade and Industry has cited the costs of poor quality as between 5% and 25% of company turnover – though no-one has attempted to produce comparative data for local government.

Tom Peters

Tom Peters is not a quality guru as such. His prolific writings cover just about every aspect of management it is possible to list – plus a number which no-one else has thought about. But a constant theme running through much of his work is the need for private and public sector organisations to be customer-centred and to provide excellent service – in a word, to focus on quality. In his book, *Thriving on Chaos*,[6] he develops this theme by describing "the attributes of a quality revolution":

- **Management obsessed with quality.** Peters emphasises that quality programmes and systems will not be effective unless top management is emotionally committed to quality and are seen consistently to place quality issues at the top of the organisational agenda.

- **There is a guiding system or ideology.** Use a quality system, says Peters. It may be Deming's, Jurans's, Crosby's or a home grown version. "It makes little difference which system you choose among the top half dozen, so long as it is thorough and followed rigorously".
- **Quality is measured.** In line with Crosby and Feigenbaum, Peters says that the costs of poor quality must and can be measured, though he urges that this is done by the participants, not by inspectors or auditors.
- **Everyone is trained in the techniques of quality assessment.** By everyone, Peters means literally everyone from the chief executive to the humblest front-line worker. The training needed, he suggests, is in "rudimentary statistical process control, group problem-solving and interaction techniques".
- **Multi-functional teams and systems are used.** The quality case for the extensive use of multi-functional teams is that "most quality improvement opportunities lie outside the natural work group". In other words, because it is often necessary to change whole systems to obtain a quality improvement, action is often needed across a number of functions or units. So multi-functional teams help to break down the barriers between separate units or tasks.
- **There is constant stimulation.** Peters' point is that like any scheme or programme, quality improvement programmes need to be kept alive by a flow of new ideas, new targets, new rewards.
- **There is a parallel organisation structure dedicated to quality improvement.** This idea includes arrangements such as a corporate quality steering group, quality planning committees and small quality improvement groups throughout the organisation.
- **Everyone is involved, including suppliers and customers.** Again in line with Crosby, Peters considers it essential to involve external organisations throughout the whole chain of activity, tapping their ideas, identifying their needs, sharing information and collaborating on achieving improvements.
- **Quality up, costs down.** Peters is a believer in the view that it is dangerous to assume a quality/cost trade-off. He argues that "perfecting quality saves money".
- **Quality improvement is a never-ending journey.** To some extent, this point duplicates the message about constant stimulation. But additionally, the argument is that concepts and expectations of quality change over time, so what seems good today can be bettered tomorrow. The corollary is that complacency about a currently good quality product or service will result in a relative deterioration in quality as standards are raised in other organisations.

Peters closes his chapter on quality by commenting that the same basic principles apply to both the private and public sectors. He believes that with budgetary pressures on public services, "a quality revolution will allow you to have your cake and eat it: improve service delivery and cut its cost simultaneously". And if this sounds a smidgen over-optimistic in the UK context, there can surely be no quarrel with his final word: "Callousness or indifference in the delivery of an inherently helpful service destroys much of its benefit".

Value management (VM)

Value management (or value analysis or value engineering) has some close similarities to the Crosby school of quality management. It is based on the concept that the value of a product or service is determined by the relationship between its cost and its purpose. This equates to Crosby's view of quality as being relative to requirement. In other words, contrary to the implication of much of Peters' approach, neither quality nor value are absolutes. Value management also involves the detailed analysis and costing of whole systems or processes – in parallel to the holistic supplier-to-end-user concept and of the Feigenbaum emphasis on costs and savings.

The application of VM in the UK has lagged significantly behind its growth in the USA, where its use in large parts of the public sector is now mandatory. It is difficult to find a reason for this lack of either interest or knowledge, except, perhaps, that unlike TQM and other management concepts, VM has not been the subject of a management best-seller. Perhaps it needs the hype and missionary fervour of a Tom Peters or a Peter Senge before UK managers start to take notice. There are indications, however, that VM may be catching on. The UK Treasury has endorsed it as a sound method of assessing value for money, and several NHS Trusts claim to have made major savings in parallel with quality improvements through the application of VM techniques. The Audit Commission has also indicated an interest in VM as a possible aid to the assessment of value and, at the end of 1996, both the European Commission for Standardisation and the British Standards Institution were working on the definition of VM or VA standards.

Like most management techniques, the origins of VM can be traced back to the ideas of one person – even though in this instance he has not gained recognition as a first division guru. Lawrence Miles, an engineer with General Electric, developed the approach (then termed value analysis) in GE's Baltimore factory in the 1940s and it was soon adopted throughout all GE's 92 plants. From there it spread to many other companies and to the US armed services who use it to assess major capital programmes. In the military context, the Pentagon rechristened it value engineering – though this term was used more in Champy's re-engineering sense than as an implication of any restriction to purely technical matters. In 1963, another industrial manager, the unusually named Charles Byetheway of Univac, developed Miles' function/cost analysis method by inventing FAST diagrams. The acronym stands for Function Analysis System Technique and is a method of showing in diagrammatic form all the functions and costs of a complete process or system. The VM process involves:

- For each VM study, which is always of whole processes, not individual tasks, a multi-discipinary project team is set up.
- The process is analysed and its various functions or elements identified and costed, using a FAST diagram. Where quality factors cannot be measured in financial terms, quality ratings are used (i.e. 'marks out of 10').

- The team then brainstorms to produce ideas for ways of improving the value/cost equation.
- The best ideas are assessed in terms of cost-effectiveness, compliance with policy, customer requirements and any other relevant factor and the results set against the original FAST analysis.
- Assuming improvements have been identified, the new and better systems are implemented.[7]

In addition to the original work of Lawrence Miles, the technique draws on several other long-established disciplines – particularly methods study and cost accounting. It links these with the whole-process concept of many of the well-known gurus and, in producing ideas for improvement, harnesses the imagination and enthusiasm of people in a team context. In this, it links a somewhat mechanistic approach to up-to-date human resource theories about the benefits of multi-functional team working and the constructive liberation of people's imagination through activities such as brainstorming.

TQM for local authorities

Quality management in a local authority is a much more complex issue than it is for a manufacturing company in which the main emphasis is on the elimination of defects. What is quality in the context of many local authority services? Quality has different meanings for different services. For physical processes such as grounds maintenance and refuse collection, specific measurable quality standards can be specified and monitored, whether the work is undertaken in-house or outsourced. For some administrative functions like council tax collection or payroll, similarly statistical and financial standards can be set. In these types of functions, the TQM principles of zero errors and of quality equating to compliance with requirements can be applied directly. The matter becomes more complicated in services in which, from the customer's or citizen's viewpoint, quality is a matter of less readily measurable factors such as politeness, helpfulness and the exercise of shrewd or imaginative judgement. A first step in developing a quality-oriented authority is for each service and function to define what quality actually consists of. If it cannot at least be described (though not necessarily measured statistically) 'quality' will be little more than an airy and ambiguous concept, interpreted differently by different interest groups.

There is a further complication if, in line with the exhortation of most quality gurus, quality is always assessed from the customers' angle. Many of the decisions and actions a local authority has to make will be applauded by some citizens and objected to by others. How, for example, should Winchester City Council target and assess the quality of its extensive traffic calming and residents' parking schemes which in 1996 generated praise from one section of the population and fierce criticism from others? There are probably answers to this, but they will not be anything like as simple or measurable as many of the private sector examples in the management literature.

The problem is that in many cases, the softer or 'fuzzy' quality factors are more important than those which are readily measurable. But if attention is concentrated on the numbers alone – as is the case with many of the Audit Commission's performance indicators – quality may appear to be good when in reality it is poor. Take planning. In terms of performance indicators, a great deal is made of the speed of processing planning applications: 95% completed within eight weeks is excellent, 50% is bad – and of course, minimising delays in processing is one aspect of quality. What this type of analysis does not reveal, however, is anything about the quality of the planning decisions – which in the longer term is considerably more important than knocking a fortnight off the processing time. An internal example is the common use in service level agreements of response times. A legal or personnel department will commit itself to answering all requests from service departments for advice within, say, two working days. That is fine as far as it goes – but what about the quality of the advice? It would seem, therefore, that local authorities would do well to avoid relying to too great an extent on those elements of TQM which emphasise detailed measurement.

Quality assurance systems, such as those which are required for BS 5750/ ISO 9000 are another matter, though even here, an over-reliance on the mechanics of a quality process is not a total guarantee of a quality service. The BS/ISO systems require a considerable amount of documentation and keeping all the records in order can too easily become an end in itself. It should also be kept in mind that these systems are not designed to produce high quality. Their purpose, very much in line with the heart of Deming's ideas, is to ensure consistency of quality standards or, as Deming put it, to minimise variability. A BS 5750 system is just as effective in guaranteeing the consistent production of crap as it is to ensure unvarying Rolls Royce quality. That said, there is a lot in Tom Peters' very pragmatic advice that it does not make much difference what quality system you use so long as you use one. And by a quality system, he meant any systematic process for defining, setting, achieving and monitoring quality standards. The implication for local authorities is that because each service has its own very individual characteristics, each service should probably evolve its own system. Effective procedures in social services to ensure a high quality of decision-making about the assessment and delivery of care for the elderly are unlikely to bear much resemblance to those needed in the fire service to prevent alleged errors of judgement leading to multi-million pound claims for damages from the owners of burnt-down factories.

However, there is a lot more to the gurus' TQM messages than the costing of errors and use of formal quality control or assurance systems. Almost all the gurus place greater emphasis on the need to develop a quality culture in which everyone in the organisation is attitudinally dedicated to high quality and the achievement of quality improvements. Most say that without this cultural context, even quality systems which are sound in principle will not be effective. Some over-enthusiastic followers of Deming or Tom Peters have gone as far as saying that if the culture is right, quality will result automatically without the need for a formal framework of supportive procedures. The problem with this view is not that culture is unimportant – it is vital – but that it fails to address the question as to how such a culture can be created. As Tom Peters points out, exhortations and slogans ('we are a quality authority') are worse than useless: they generate cynicism among employees and service users. What is evident from writers on culture (see chapter 7) is that cultural change has to be planned and managed, and that a wide range of supportive measures are needed to influence attitudes and reinforce the targeted cultural values. It is also important to recognise that publicity about quality initiatives raises public expectations about standards. What was accepted yesterday becomes unacceptable tomorrow, once an authority has announced its quality ambitions or publicised its award of a Chartermark. Quality systems had better deliver.

It follows that a local authority which includes continuous quality improvement as one of its core and cultural values, will need to combine the cultural and systems approaches and develop a quality strategy which includes principles drawn from a wider range of sources as well as from the quality gurus. There are elements in the management theories outlined in all the chapters of this book which can contribute to the achievement of quality objectives. Taking this broad view of the subject, the most significant factors are probably:

- **The emphasis on whole processes or systems.** Many of the more major needs and opportunities for quality improvements require action in more than one function or unit, or to more than one procedure. For example, to improve the quality of the housing benefit activity, far more may be needed than just making the application forms more user-friendly. It may require a collaborative effort involving at least three separate departments – housing, finance and social services.
- **The need to view the authority's activities from a user or citizen viewpoint** and therefore to have systems and structures in place which develop contacts with the outside world and give the community and special interest groups a voice. For many services, the characteristics of good quality are not those a professional officer would list but the rather more down-to-earth judgements made by services users.
- **The need for some kind of supportive system,** and the influence of quality as a core 7-S value. It may be that value management, with its rather curious blend of old-fashioned method study and cost/benefit analysis with the more modern ideas of multi-functional teams and brainstorming, is particularly well suited to the public sector. It does not involve so extreme a culture shock as launching Japanese-flavoured kaizen programmes. But more is needed than a single quality system. Quality as a value needs to permeate the whole authority, including:
  — quality improvement targets in collective and individual performance objectives and appraisal;
  — procedures and events which encourage all employees to contribute their knowledge and ideas to the improvement of quality;

— using activities like team briefings and staff training to promote the quality message and develop any necessary new skills.

- **Top management as role models,** demonstrating by attitude and action that they believe in the importance of quality – a factor which has links with the next chapter.

Footnotes:
1. *Total Quality: Success through people*, Ron Collard, IPM, 1993.
2. *The Deming Management Method*, Mary Walton, Mercury Books, 1989.
3. *Quality Without Tears*, Phillip Crosby, New American Library, 1984.
4. *Total Quality Control*, Armand Feigenbaum, McGraw Hill, 1983.
5. *Encyclopaedic Dictionary of Organisational Behaviour*, Nigel Nicholson (Ed.), Blackwell, 1995.
6. *Thriving on Chaos*, Tom Peters, Macmillan, 1987.
7. *Modern Quality Management Manual*, Clive Bone, Longman, 1994.

Chapter 11

Leadership theories

The historical background

People have been studying, theorising and writing about leadership for centuries. James Burns, one of the leadership gurus this chapter will be discussing, has commented that leadership is "one of the most observed and least understood phenomena on earth" – probably because there has always been a mixture of fascination and bafflement about the necessary qualities for successful leadership. Machiavelli had no doubts about this. From his 16th century perspective, to survive and succeed as a leader, the qualities needed were cunning, pragmatism, intelligence, charm and ruthlessness. One need only substitute the word 'leader' for 'prince' in quotations from his famous work *The Prince*,[1] to show how Machiavelli was prepared to write more honestly about the realities of some forms of successful leadership than most modern gurus would ever dare. For example, after commending qualities such as honesty and integrity, Machiavelli went on:

> "A (leader) need not necessarily have all the good qualities I mentioned above, but he should certainly appear to have them... He should appear to be compassionate, faithful to his word, guileless and devout. And indeed he should be so. But his disposition should be such that, if he needs to be the opposite, he knows how... He should not deviate from what is good, if that is possible, but he should know how to do evil, if that is necessary".

Underlying Machiavelli's ideas was a profoundly negative view of what makes people tick. He thought everyone was out to further their own individual interests and that no-one could be trusted to behave honourably or with concern for others. So carrots and sticks were needed, and the leader just had to be more cunning than the led. He justified the devious prince who sometimes broke his promises with the pessimistic statement that: "because men are wretched creatures who would not keep their word to you, you need not keep your word to them". Machiavelli and FW Taylor would have got on fine, though managers who enjoy playing organisational politics and want to improve the relevant skills will find Machiavelli by far the best tutor.

Now jump four centuries to the late 1940s and early 1950s. Leadership in an industrial context was then a very live issue throughout all the countries which were facing the task of converting from military to civilian outputs, or – as in Germany and Japan – attempting to rebuild their war-shattered factories and economies. What sort of men (hardly anyone then thought of women in a top management context) were needed to lead the huge changes involved? The apparently obvious model was the successful military leader – the Eisenhowers, Montgomerys and Pattons. If you can beat the Germans at El Alamein by a heady mixture of shrewd planning and personal charisma, surely the same factors would guarantee success in industrial civvy street. A number of academics and other writers consequently studied the great World War Two commanders and produced long lists of leadership qualities which combined what they saw as the most effective aspects of all of them. It was gradually realised that there were two major problems with this approach:

- Some of the successful leaders were so different that it was impossible to reconcile their very different styles. General Patton was tough, gung-ho, a large-scale risk taker. General Montgomery was a careful planner who tried to minimise risk. General Eisenhower was a charmer: the idea of charm would have made Bomber Harris sick. Orde Wingate was a maverick... and so on. Successful leaders stubbornly refused to fit into a nice neat box.
- This did not stop the theorists producing their lists of qualities of the ideal leader. The problem here, however, was that about the only person capable of meeting these criteria was the Angel Gabriel. The combination of intelligence, wit, sensitivity, resilience, integrity, imagination, practicality, vision, inspiration, courage and a dozen more desirable qualities, would probably make a good leader – but who could aspire to such a pinnacle of perfection?

In the next two decades, attention moved away from the personality characteristics of effective leaders towards the design of management systems and the processes of leadership – what good leaders do, rather than what they are. As a phrase, 'leadership' almost disappeared from management literature and was substituted by 'management'. Two themes were developed:

- The idea that insofar as leadership was still relevant, different situations called for different leadership styles. Leadership, in a word, was situational. For example, leading a design team of highly trained specialists on an extremely complex technical assignment was seen to call for very different qualities from the leader of a go-getting sales team.
- The view that impersonal systems – particularly management by objectives – could achieve more consistent results than reliance on managers' individual leadership qualities.

From the perspective of the 1990s, the first of these themes has had the more enduring impact, although the importance of systems to provide a framework for less readily definable managerial activity is a constant theme throughout all the subjects discussed in this book.

The 1980s and 1990s have seen the rise to fame of several management gurus, specialising in leadership studies, and putting forward both new ideas and more sophisticated spin to the concepts of previous decades. The principal, though by no means only players, are:

- The British leadership guru, John Adair, and his theory of Action Centred Leadership.
- Tom Peters, who although a generalist has always placed a central emphasis on the importance of inspirational leadership.
- Sir John Harvey Jones, the past chairman of ICI and now television personality, with his very personal philosophy of the leader as conductor of the organisational orchestra.
- Warren Bennis, the American psychologist and management academic, the leading leadership guru, who makes a major distinction between management and leadership.
- James Burns, another American guru, who first developed the terminology and concepts of transactional and transformational leadership – the latter being very much in vogue in the late 1990s, despite having first been described in the USA by Burns in 1978. In brief, the theory is that transactional leadership is based on securing compliance; transformational leadership achieves commitment.

Action centred leadership

The resurgence of interest in leadership at the end of the 1970s was exemplified by Surrey University establishing a chair in leadership studies in 1979, and appointing John Adair to this position. Adair, who has a military background, believes that leadership can be taught – that it involves skills which can be learnt, rather than being an innate aptitude. He claims that his concept of leadership is not unique in any particular element, but differs from that of other writers and practitioners by integrating ideas from many sources into a single and essentially practical leadership model. This one aspect of this model reflects much earlier research in the USA by Rensis Likert, which indicated that the least effective supervisors were 'job-centred', in contrast to those with the best records who were 'employee-centred'. Adair also draws on both the transactional and transformational theories (without actually using these terms) in his 'Fifty Fifty Rule'. This suggests that half an individual's motivation at work comes from internal drives (transformational) and half from external influences (transactional).

As a result of synthesizing a range of leadership theories, together with his own experience in the armed services, Adair produced his concept of Action Centred Leadership, which has become sufficiently widely applied to have earned the ultimate accolade of an acronym – ACL. The concept is based on the view that leadership implies team working and that it is both natural and necessary for a team to have a leader. The ACL idea is illustrated by three overlapping circles labelled Task, Team and Individual. This suggests that any working group has three basic requirements:

- To be successful in achieving its tasks.
- To maintain social cohesion as a team of mutually supportive members.
- To be aware of, and help to satisfy, the individual needs of its members.

The three circles are overlapping because success or failure in any one affects the other two. Action-centred leadership involves ensuring a unifying balance between these three aspects.

Although the social and psychological elements of leadership are given prominence in this model (the team and individual circles), ACL has had a strong appeal to many managers because of its complementary emphasis on task achievement. The fact that ACL is taught at Sandhurst and has been promoted for many years by the Industrial Society, is evidence of its practical appeal. There are literally thousands of supervisors and managers, including many in local government, who have been on short ACL courses and who now carry a little plastic card in their wallets showing the three circles and a few bullet points of advice about putting ACL into practice. Those who want to dig more deeply into John Adair's approach will find the basic ACL theory in his first book in 1983, *Effective Leadership*, and more about individuals and teams in his 1990 text, *Understanding Motivation*.[2]

The Tom Peters leadership philosophy

In Tom Peters' first book after *In Search of Excellence* – *A Passion for Excellence* – he worked himself up to a fine old lather about the inadequacies of much industrial leadership. Discard the manager and replace with the leader, was the message. In a talk given around this time to a local government conference in Bournemouth he went as far as declaiming that he despised the word management. Managers should stop managing and start leading, and the leader, to quote from the book and the lecture, had to be "an enthusiast, nurturer of champions, hero-finder, wanderer, dramatist, coach, facilitator, builder". It is tempting to add 'walker on water', and at least some of the 600 local authority managers must have left Bournemouth feeling marginally inadequate.

In his next book, *Thriving on Chaos*,[3] Peters had calmed down enough to produce a more detailed set of ideas about effective leadership and had allowed 'management' to reappear in his vocabulary. His approach in this book had four main elements:

- The effective leader continually challenges conventional methods and wisdom, and achieves constant change in response to the continuously changing environment.
- Three leadership tools can be used to establish organisational and team direction and commitment:
  — having a clear view or vision as to what the organisation is there for, and communicating this to everyone with enthusiasm;
  — managing by example: recognising that everyone in an organisation is a boss-watcher;

- — being highly visible and keeping in touch – 'management by wandering about'.
- Effective leaders encourage and empower people to take the initiative in a drive for continuous improvement. This has four dimensions:
  - — being a good listener: getting people to talk about their perceptions of work and paying attention to their ideas;
  - — giving a priority to front-line workers – those in direct contact with the customer;
  - — maximising delegation within clearly defined values and standards;
  - — pursuing horizontal management: encouraging collaborative working across functions and units.
- Effective leaders learn to love change, and develop a change culture by:
  - — evaluating everyone's performance by the extent to which they make changes to the way they do things;
  - — generating a sense of urgency throughout the organisation about the need to respond, adapt and improve.

This is still a very formidable schedule, but Peters' book did offer some detailed advice about what managers might do on a day-to-day basis to develop these leadership behaviours. This included spending 75% of time out of the office, talking frequently and informally to staff and customers, keeping a notebook to record points raised in these conversations and always responding to these persons' concerns and ideas, using stories and special events to get the organisation's message across, and abolishing status symbols like the reserved car parking space.

Advice from the Troubleshooter

It says something about how the British value top managers that as Chairman of ICI, Sir John Harvey Jones was a name hardly known outside business circles, whereas when he retired and fronted the television series, *Troubleshooter*, he soon achieved star status. Since then, he has joined the ranks of the world's highly sought after conference speakers, as well as writing several books about management which are widely available on station and airport bookstalls.

Sir John is the odd man out among the gurus included in this book for being the only one to have headed a major industrial corporation and to have no academic connections. He went to the Royal Naval College at the age of 13, stayed in the Navy until after the war, and then joined ICI as a work study officer. From there, he steadily worked his way up the ICI hierarchy until, somewhat to his own surprise, he reached the top. His appeal to many managers (apart from his dazzling ties) is partly that he has extensive practical experience of what he is talking about and partly his very natural modesty and good humour.

It is not surprising that his views about leadership are essentially practical and make little reference to the academic literature. Much of what he says, however, can be related to leadership theory, and to a blend of transactional and transformational styles. His metaphor for the effective leader is the conductor of an orchestra – someone who can achieve nothing on their own and who has to get results by co-ordinating and inspiring the efforts of others. The concept is developed in detail in his book, *All Together Now* – though the same approach runs through earlier books such as *Making it Happen* and *Getting it Together*.

Underlying Sir John's philosophy is a profound belief that 'ordinary' people have far more potential than most organisations are ever able to release. The job of the manager as leader, therefore, is to create an environment in which people will willingly give of their best. He has some very harsh words to say about some common management attitudes or assumptions. For example:

> "I am by nature a mild-mannered man who likes to consider himself tolerant and understanding; however, when people are referred to as 'human resources' and are evaluated in the same way as money, raw materials or technology, a red haze settles over my eyes".

Or again:

> "The whole concept of management in Britain has been debased by being seen as synonymous with control and regulation... We simply have to find ways of switching people on rather than turning people off".[4]

Most of Sir John's advice about effective leadership flows almost automatically from his belief in the latent capabilities and positive attitudes of people, and from his view that it is the people who are actually doing a job who know most about it and are therefore in the best position to suggest how it might be improved. No manager who has a strong and genuine set of such beliefs would feel comfortable acting in a macho or autocratic manner, emphasising status distinctions, failing to communicate, ignoring the views of front-line staff, never applauding good work, or using mistakes solely to allocate blame.

To some extent, anyone sharing Sir John's beliefs about human nature should have little difficulty in adopting a leadership style (in terms of everyday management behaviour) which displays the reverse of these negative characteristics. If you really believe that front-line staff have a lot to offer, you will go and talk with them. If you truly believe that people respond to recognition and praise, you will make sure you give it. If you genuinely believe that mistakes can be a powerful source of learning, you will not allow a culture of blame to develop. If your view is that many conventional status distinctions create attitudinal barriers between managers and their staff, you will not have 'chief officers only' painted across a privileged strip of parking spaces or, heaven help us, hold a key to the executive loo.

But Sir John's ideas are not all reliant on being optimistic about human nature. As an experienced manager, he also offers a good deal of common-sense advice about supportive systems and practices. Among these are:

- Develop and promote a realistic and relevant set of values. "The values which

permeate an organisation from top to bottom produce the invisible framework which substitutes for continual control and perennial hands-on
meddling with tiny details".

- Do not use overly prescriptive job descriptions which place too close a limit
  on people's freedom to act and innovate – provided there is clarity about
  accountability for results and about essential standards.
- Treat 'management by walking about' as simply a normal way of managing
  – not as an additional task or technique.
- "On a scale of sticks and carrots, there should be about 10 carrots to every
  stick".
- Develop coaching skills – particularly for use with young or inexperienced
  staff.
- Give a high priority to all forms of training and learning.
- Minimise chains of communication and command by developing flat, non-
  hierarchical organisational structures.
- Make extensive use of teams, and select team members with care to ensure a
  productive mix of skills and styles.
- Do not place much confidence in performance-related pay as a motivator.
  What is more important is recognition of good work, and discussion (in an
  appraisal context) about work objectives and outcomes.
- Do not duck the need on occasion to issue reproofs or to dismiss, but do so
  fairly and without personal antagonism.

Warren Bennis: leaders not managers

In the USA, and probably internationally, Warren Bennis has the reputation of
being in the first division, if not the leader, of leadership gurus. He is an industrial
psychologist, academic and management author and journalist, who has also acted
as an adviser to four American presidents. He has based most of his extensive writings on leadership on studies of actual leaders in different walks of life, including
orchestral conductors, sports coaches, company executives, politicians and astro-
nauts. In perhaps his most widely read book, *Leaders: the Strategies for Taking
Charge*, published in 1985,[5] he claimed he had identified four key leadership
competencies:

- **The management of attention** – by which he meant the ability to obtain the
  interest and commitment of people to the leader's vision.
- **The management of meaning** – the ability to communicate clearly and to help
  people understand how the vision could be converted to reality.
- **The management of trust** – achieved by the leader securing admiration, if not
  always agreement, for their obvious consistency of purpose. (UK readers will
  have their own views about Bennis' choice of Margaret Thatcher as an
  example).
- **The management of self** – a willingness by the leader to go on learning,
  coupled with the ability to make a shrewd assessment of personal strengths,
  weaknesses and learning needs.

Bennis has also described what he labels as the 'basic ingredients' of leadership:

- The posession of a guiding vision – having a clear idea about you want to do plus the strength to persist in this aim, regardless of setbacks or obstacles.
- A passion for your particular vocation or occupation – loving what you do.
- Integrity – consisting of a blend of self-knowledge, candour and maturity.
- Curiosity – a continual interest in new ideas and a willingness to go on learning.
- Daring – a willingness to take risks and to learn from mistakes.

The most widely quoted of Bennis' aphorisms is: 'Managers do things right: leaders do the right thing' – a saying which like many popular management sayings can be criticised for grossly over-simplifying the realities of real life. It gives the impression that managing and leading are two different roles – a view which would almost certainly bring another red haze to the eyes of Sir John Harvey Jones. But before setting it aside, it is worth examining other differences which Bennis distinguishes between leadership and management. In summarised form, Bennis says differences include:

- Managers administrate: leaders innovate.
- Managers are copies: leaders are originals.
- Managers focus on systems and structures: leaders focus on people.
- Managers control: leaders generate trust.
- Managers address the short term: leaders address the long term.
- Managers focus on the bottom line: leaders look to the horizon.
- Managers accept the status quo: leaders challenge it.
- Managers are classic good soldiers: leaders are their own persons.

All this is more a Tom Peters' view, than Sir John's or John Adair's, because it seems to imply that the essence of leadership lies in the personal qualities and attitudes of the leader rather than in any type of learnable skill or management practice. It may seem odd, therefore, that Bennis also stresses that leadership can be learnt, and it may be significant that he has been strongly criticised by John Adair for over-emphasising the idea that becoming an effective leader is dependent on self-fulfilment. Self-fulfilment, says Adair, may be a by-product of becoming a leader – not the means of doing it.

Transactional v transformational leadership

In what is probably a perpetual debate about leadership, much attention has recently been given to ideas first propounded by James Macgregor Burns in the USA back in 1978. Burns distinguished two main types of leadership:

- Leaders who value their followers and reward them for achieving the leader's objectives – Burns termed this transactional leadership, because it involves an unwritten transaction between the leader and the followers. Followers understand that in exchange for their effort and achievement, they will benefit in some way – not necessarily financially, but by such means as the value of additional experience, the acquisition of new skills, or personal satisfaction.

- Leaders who create a vision, shared with their followers, which generates enthusiasm and commitment for its own sake. Burns' term for this was transformational leadership, because it involves changing (transforming) followers' attitudes and motivation.

This somewhat abstract or philosophical concept has since been expanded into a more detailed and practical approach. An emerging UK leadership specialist (not quite at guru level) who is using this more developed approach, both in her research and in management training, is Dr Beverley Allimo-Metcalfe of the Nuffield Institute. In a talk to a local government conference early in 1996, she described the characteristics of transformational leadership which had emerged from research in the USA and UK. The US research indicated that the principal characteristics were:

- Having a strong sense of vision and the ability to articulate this.
- A degree of personal charisma, in the sense of being able to enthuse and inspire.
- The ability to stimulate new thinking.
- A genuine concern for individuals.

The UK research had produced a slightly different list:

- The ability to inspire commitment to a shared vision and values.
- Challenging current processes – not accepting past practice.
- Enabling others to act – developing a sense of shared 'ownership' of issues.
- Role modelling – demonstrating personal commitment to the organisation's values.
- Recognising and celebrating achievement.

Transactional leadership, in her view, was the established style which emphasised planning, analysis, logic and the creation of order. Her research suggested a gender bias, with male managers tending strongly towards the transactional and women managers adopting a more transformational style. She accepted, however, that there were circumstances in which the transactional style was appropriate. Transformational managers often had the capacity to adopt the transactional approach when necessary, but transactional managers found difficulty in switching into a transformational role. Her advice on how to develop in a transformational direction was:

- Seek feedback on your own performance, especially from subordinates.
- Know and make clear the limits of any compromise.
- Articulate values and be consistent with them in your own conduct.
- Develop leaders among your subordinates.
- Find personal mentors, and act as a mentor for others.

An emerging European guru, Professor Manfred Kets de Vries of the international Insead business school, is a strong advocate of the transformational approach. He is an outspoken critic of what he describes as the narcissism and hypocrisy of many business leaders who defend 'obscene pay levels' and mouth platitudes about people being their most valued resource. Asked by one chief executive for advice on maintaining staff morale during a company's downsizing programme, he says his answer was: 'Go hang yourself!'. Other sayings of his include: 'The moment you become a leader you are surrounded by liars'; 'Every leader needs a fool'; and 'The only person who welcomes change is a wet baby'.

On a more positive basis, his list of qualities of the transformational leader include pragmatic idealism, a commitment to developing people, performance orientation, tolerance of mistakes, open-mindedness, speed of action, and a sense of fun.

Leadership in local authorities

Whatever the difficulties of defining just what effective leadership is, it is obvious from everyday observation that the style and effectiveness of local authorities, like any other organisation, is very strongly influenced by members and managers who are in leadership roles. Many senior managers will say they owe much of their current career success to the earlier experience of working for an outstanding director or chief executive. Most of the authorities which have acquired a widely acknowledged reputation for excellence have equally respected top managers and political leaders at the helm. What is not always given sufficient attention is that effective leadership is not just an issue for chief executives and directors – all supervisors and managers, at all levels and throughout all services, have a leadership role.

What can everyone who has responsibility for other people learn from the leadership gurus? Perhaps the first point is to avoid thinking of management and leadership as two separate activities. One of the most irritating features of some gurus' theories (not only in relation to leadership) is to present different views as mutually exclusive rather than as complementary. Contrary to the implications of Bennis' analysis, managers have to be leaders and leaders have to manage. Leaders need to generate enthusiasm and commitment: they also need to clarify objectives and ensure necessary things get done – and this implies working in both the transactional and transformational modes.

In the local government context, the duality of leadership – political and managerial – also needs to be recognised. It is dangerous, not just confusing, if the chief executive has one vision for the authority and the political leadership another. In the development and articulation of vision and values – which all the gurus agree is central to effective leadership – there needs to be a common understanding and a consistent message. At the same time, it is important to distinguish between the political and managerial leadership role. As Professor Alan Whitehead of Southampton Institute (and past Labour leader of Southampton City Council) has pointed out in several seminar talks, the political leader often has a need for short term successes within the electoral cycle in order to gain support for longer term aims. Officers must understand these political dynamics and not interpret them as in conflict with strategic proposals developed with the managerial leadership.

In addition, the political leader's colleagues, unlike the managerial leader's subordinates, cannot be dismissed for incompetence. The political leader must make the best out of whatever combination of talents and personalities the electoral process throws up. Trade-offs (hopefully only in the metaphorical sense) may also be necessary to secure support among a political leader's colleagues for particular policies or decisions. The implication of Professor Whitehead's views is that political leadership has, by necessity, to be rather more Machiavellian than managerial leadership, and managers should understand and accept this, rather than criticising members for sometimes concentrating on detailed short-term issues and indulging in a certain amount of wheeler-dealing.

For managers, the key points emerging from an otherwise confusing range of leadership literature are:

- The importance of shared values and their explanation and promotion throughout the authority (back to 7-S!).
- The need for leader-managers to be highly visible – to be out and about, talking with their staff (and customers) and listening to their staff's concerns, views and ideas.
- Encouraging staff to put forward ideas for improvements and to try out new ways of working; coupled with a tolerance of honest mistakes and the avoidance of a blame culture when mistakes occur.
- Being genuinely committed to helping staff develop their skills and realise their potential, and giving practical support through the provision of training, the use of opportunities for gaining more experienced, personal coaching and the encouragement of mentoring.
- Consistency of personal style and conduct – not friendly and conversational one day and remote and formal the next.
- The positive recognition of good work and the celebration (and therefore reinforcement) of success – if by no more sophisticated means than taking the team out for a meal or giving an individual a personally written note saying thank you and well done.
- Clarity about essential standards and any no-go issues such as bullying or the acceptance of gifts from contractors. The effective leader is not soft when it comes to maintaining necessary standards or correcting unacceptable behaviour.
- Acting as a role model – both in behaving in accordance with the authority's values and in acting managerially as you would wish more junior managers to behave.
- Never falling back simply on status to justify a decision – always explaining the reasons.
- Extensive staff communication and information, explaining the whole context in which decisions and actions have to be made, not just the details of those elements which apply specifically to the staff concerned.
- Being as open and honest about bad news as about good.
- The avoidance of prevarication – staff have little respect for leaders who cannot make up their minds.
- Being committed to personal continuing development.

It is all too easy to be discouraged by the emphasis given by some gurus to the innate personality characteristics of high profile leaders. No amount of training will create the mysterious quality of charisma or convert the pragmatist into an evangelising idealist. But this does not mean that it is impossible to become more competent as a leader. There are many supervisors and managers throughout local government who obtain the respect and commitment of their teams in a quiet, undramatic manner, in which clarity of direction, honesty, and concern and respect for others comprise the major components. More can sometimes be learned about effective leadership by observing the experienced, respected but probably low status supervisor than by trying to copy the idiosyncrasies of local government's equivalents in the upper echelons of Churchill or Montgomery (not to mention Hitler).

Footnotes:
1. *The Prince*, Niccolo Machiavelli, translated by George Bull, Folio Press, 1970.
2. *Effective Leadership*, John Adair, Pan, 1993 and *Understanding Motivation*, John Adair, Talbot Adair (distributed by Kogan Page), 1990.
3. *Thriving on Chaos*, Tom Peters, Macmillan, 1988.
4. *All Together Now*, Sir John Harvey Jones, Heinemann, 1994.
5. *Leaders: the strategies for taking charge*, Walter Bennis, Harper and Row, 1985.

Chapter 12

A miscellany of gurus

Each of the previous chapters examines the ideas of various management gurus in relation to a specific topic. In some cases, such as business process re-engineering and the learning organisation, the topic and its buzzword have been the product of single gurus who are recognised as the 'owners' of the concept and who may have had little to say about any other aspects of management. In other cases, while the origins of a management concept can be traced to one particular guru, others have developed these original ideas and added their own concepts as part of a wide range of management thinking. Thus a few gurus, such as Michael Hammer and Peter Senge, have come to fame as single issue thinkers: others – and Peter Drucker and Tom Peters are prime examples – have written and spoken on every aspect of management under the sun. For those in this latter category, this book has been highly selective by focusing only on what they have said about the particular topic which forms the subject of each chapter. This final chapter takes a different approach. It looks briefly at some of the ideas and sayings of the all-purpose gurus on topics not addressed in chapters 1 to 11, but which seem to have some relevance to UK local authorities in the late 1990s.

Peter Drucker on managing public services

Most of the best known gurus make occasional reference to the public sector but their main concern has been (and remains) the diagnosis of factors leading to the success of companies operating in an increasingly competitive, international business environment. Peter Drucker is no exception so far as the vast majority of his very extensive writings are concerned, but in one of his many books there is a chapter on *Managing the Public Service Institution.*[1]

Topically, although written about the USA over 20 years ago, it starts by commenting that public service organisations have come under increasing criticism for poor quality services, their demand for an increasing proportion of the national wealth, and bureaucratic insensitivity. Drucker noted that the response of the public sector to these criticisms had been to attempt to become more management conscious, and that to do so, public institutions had turned to the business world to learn about management tools and techniques.

Despite the relevance of concepts such as management by objectives (of which Drucker is a great fan), he considered this had led to three misconceived explanations for the shortcomings of public service institutions:

- That they were not sufficiently 'businesslike'.
- That they needed to employ better quality people.
- That their objectives were too intangible.

Sounds familiar? Drucker appears to be echoing precisely the criticisms which have encouraged some local authority leaders and chief executives to run councils as though they were plcs. The enthusiasts for behaving like a business will be surprised to discover that Drucker – otherwise a high priest of private sector entrepreneurialism – thinks they are dangerously mistaken. His chapter goes on:

> "The popular view is that the public service institution will perform only if it is managed in a 'businesslike' manner... But it is the wrong diagnosis... The service institution has performance troubles precisely because it is not a business. What being businesslike usually means in a service institution is little more than the control of cost... But the basic problem of service institutions is not high cost but lack of effectiveness. They may be very efficient. But they tend then not to do the right things... Costs may go down. But services essential to the institution's purpose may be slighted or lopped off in the name of efficiency".

Drucker then shoots down the idea that the public sector requires higher quality people, or that the appointment of business leaders to head public service institutions is any solution. Effective business people, he says, become bureaucrats almost overnight when they head a service function. Public sector managers, he goes on, are no less competent, qualified or hard-working than their private sector counterparts and if service institutions cannot be run by people of normal endowment they cannot be run at all.

Drucker accepts that the most plausible reason for poor public sector performance is the intangibility of their objectives – but he considers this at best only a half-truth. It all depends on how intangible criteria are translated into practical targets. He suggests as an example, the intangible objective of a school being "the development of the whole personality" – a legitimate but unmeasurable aim. But its delivery can be supported by evolving related measurable targets such as ensuring all children can read by completion of the third grade.

Drucker suggests six requirements for success in a public service organisation:

1. Define the organisation's primary function – what it is there for. What service institutions need is not to be more business-like. He says a hospital needs to be more 'hospital-like' (NHS please note) and a governmental body more 'government-like'.

2. Identify clear objectives and goals from the definition of function and mission. Ensure an emphasis on achieving the right results – doing the right thing (effectiveness), not simply efficiency.
3. Define priorities, set standards and deadlines, ensure clarity of accountability for results.
4. Define relevant measurements of performance – including ways of assessing qualitative factors such as customer satisfaction.
5. Use feedback from these measurements – "build self-control from results into the system".
6. Institute a systematic review to identify and 'slough off' objectives which are no longer relevant or attainable. Drucker says this may be the most important point of the six. The absence of the test of commercial success or failure may, he suggests, result in public sector organisations continuing to put time and resources into programmes or services which have outlived their relevance. Knowing when to stop is as important as the launch of new initiatives.

In general, Drucker's advice is to use the private sector's management tools and techniques, but make sure they are directed towards public service aims and values. He would certainly be critical of authorities which have allowed CCT to divert their aims away from the governmental and community representational roles towards winning and keeping in-house contracts on the basis of 'business-like' cost and profit targets. Authorities should aim to be more 'local government-like', not more like companies.

Tom Peters on himself

For many UK managers, the first name they will think of if asked to name a management guru is Tom Peters. But ask them to summarise his central message or theme and you will either receive very different answers from different managers, or be met with a baffled silence. Ten years ago, the reply would probably have been 'excellence', but since then, Peters has written and lectured in an increasingly unstructured manner on more organisational and managerial topics than a bevy of business graduates could shake a collective stick at. Boiled down to its essence, however, Tom Peters' message is inseparable from the way he communicates it. In the words of Marshal McLuhan, the medium is the message – the medium in this case being TP himself.

This is not to imply that his ideas lack substance or to deny that for many managers, Peters has been a source of inspiration – and inspiration is a key word. Peters has an outstanding ability to generate excitement and enthusiasm for managing better, and to jolt complacent managers into questioning whether they are as good as they think they are. To do so in print, he fills his books with exaggerated or provocative statements such as: 'you can become excellent in a nano-second', 'don't even think about getting it "right" ', 'the customer comes second', or 'leap then look'. In person, he uses the same technique with the added impact of a style of delivery like the evangelist Billy Graham on speed. Managers who attend his seminars – and this has included hundreds of UK local authority officers – come away with a real buzz. Two hours of Tom Peters is the equivalent for many people of a high boost battery charge. As the blurb to one of his latest books puts it: "You've got to take that leap, then leap again – catapult their imaginations, blow their mindsets, knock their Nikes off!"[2]

Is there any relevance to UK local authorities in the Peters gospel? What he is really preaching is a personal philosophy which, if accepted, is applicable to anyone in any sector. It is a view that work in any type of organisation is, or should be, exciting and fun, provided one accepts three things:

- That external influences and the effects of organisational decisions are increasingly unpredictable – hence 'thriving on chaos'.
- That most people, particularly staff in the front-line, have enormous potential which is rarely tapped because of hierarchical restrictions and rigid systems of conventionally structured organisations.
- That there are no right or simple answers. As Peters says: "An awful lot of people come to my seminars looking for answers. Thanks for coming, but there are no answers. Just an awful lot of questions…" Or again: "Beware of easy solutions and 'rules' laid down by management gurus, starting with yours truly".[3]

For managers, what Peters is apparently saying is: don't get hooked on any management technique as the best way of doing anything; manage in whatever way you find most satisfying provided you respect other people; and try to have fun doing it. In his own words: "*Joi de vivre*. That's what an ordinary day at work ought to be about. Why not eh?".

Sir John Harvey-Jones on performance-related pay (PRP)

Unlike many management gurus, Sir John Harvey-Jones has had many years practical experience of the topics he writes about, both as a specialist in his earliest industrial job as a work study officer and later as he worked his way up through ICI's managerial hierarchy. It might be thought that with his grounding in work-study bonus schemes, and as a private sector manager with a keen interest in motivation, he would favour linking pay firmly to performance. In fact, he is very doubtful about its effectiveness and acutely aware of its potential problems.

In *All Together Now*[4] he comments that the current heavy emphasis on PRP has two causes. One is the attempt to make pay a variable so that the paybill fluctuates in line with the financial fortunes of the business: the other (and this is the main case put by local government proponents of PRP) is that performance pay provides an incentive for employees to improve their performance. Sir John's conclusion is in line with the motivational theories of Frederick Herzberg – that while unfair pay demotivates, pay itself is not a motivator.

Referring to his days as a work study officer, he acknowledges that performance bonusing can focus employees' attention on those aspects of the work to which pay is linked. But this, he says, can have two unfortunate results:

- Other aspects of the work are then given inadequate attention.

- The individual nature of most PRP systems impedes effective teamwork.

Team PRP, however, has other disadvantages. "A group performance-related pay system in which everybody receives the same percentage or bonus payment can barely be described as a motivator". Sir John concludes by saying he is dubious about the validity of any general PRP scheme. "It has to be capable of infinite gradation and consequently lands one on the endless Tibetan prayer wheel of greater and greater complexity". He favours pay systems which are transparent, so that there is no suspicion among employees of bias or other unfairness, and points to the greater motivational impact than pay of personal recognition, jointly agreed objective setting, the provision of training, and personal satisfaction for a job well done. He would, it seems, welcome the current trend for authorities which have introduced performance pay rethinking their PRP schemes. The question they should be asking is 'why have PRP?', not 'how should we operate it?'.

Ed Schein's career anchors

What makes managers stay with an organisation instead of shopping around for better jobs elsewhere? Edgar Schein, the American social psychologist who invented the psychological contract discussed in chapter 6, also developed the notion of 'career anchors'. These are the characteristics of work which encourage people to stay rather than leave.

Staff retention has not been a significant problem for local authorities during the recession, while many managers also decided to stay put until the outcome of the local government review was known. Now that the final decisions about the reorganisation shambles have at least (and at last) been made, and as the economy begins to recover, staff turnover may again become an issue authorities will have to address. Schein's career anchors will then be well worth studying, as they provide a checklist of many important factors quite apart from salary which influence people's career decisions to stay with one employer.

Schein's anchors, in summary, are set in six categories.[5] He did not suggest that all were important to all people, because individuals vary in what turns them on, but he suggested that it was factors of whichever of these kinds were important to each individual, which were a major influence in deciding whether to seek a career move:

- **For the technically or functionally minded:**
  — the opportunity to exercise particular skills,
  — a reluctance to give up particular expertise,
  — management as such not felt to be of great significance.
- **For the managerially minded:**
  — clarity of accountability for results,
  — being able to abandon a technical for a generalist role,
  — the satisfaction of co-ordinating the activities of others.
- **Autonomy:**
  — freedom from restrictive organisational rules and requirements,
  — extensive personal control of how, when and where to work.

- Security/stability:
  — perception of security in the job, in pay and in the place of work,
  — performing well in the particular type of organisation,
  — career development supported by the organisation.
- Service/dedication:
  — opportunity to achieve things which satisfy personal interests and concerns,
  — organisational values are in accord with personal values.
- Challenge:
  — opportunities to gain satisfaction from winning,
  — problems are seen as challenges to be overcome,
  — variety and novelty in the work.

The list provides a useful reminder that for many people, it is the characteristics of their work which loom largest in making career decisions, and that it should not be assumed that everyone seeks the same characteristics. In the local authority, for example, the person who gains deep satisfaction from technical or professional aspects may well begin to look elsewhere if there is a general assumption that everyone aspires to general management. The current fashion for denigrating professionalism in favour of management will provide a strong incentive for dedicated, but unmanagerial professional staff, to seek work elsewhere, to the detriment of authorities which still need high levels of specialist expertise to ensure high quality services. Characteristics of more general impact are security (in the sense of knowing how one stands) and most important, a compatibility of organisational and personal values.

Charles Handy on power

Politics in local government is usually thought of in terms of political parties. Politics in the more Machiavellian sense of how power and influence operate within the management structure may be recognised but is often frowned on. 'Too much politics' is a not uncommon managerial criticism of the wheeling, dealing and string-pulling which go on in almost every authority – and for that matter, in every type of organisation. Yet strangely, organisational politics of this kind has been rarely considered by the management gurus. Listen to Deming or Hammer, for example, and it might be thought that the key to effective management is the adoption of a single set of rational concepts and techniques. Charles Handy is one of the few management gurus who accepts the inevitability of organisational politicking and has offered some thoughts about its characteristics. In his book, *Inside Organisations*,[6] written to accompany a television series about the management of change, he says:

"It took me a long while to realise that power and politics are part of life in organisations everywhere. We have to learn to live with them and the more we understand them the better we will be able to cope".

The key word here is power, and Handy suggests there are three kinds of power which can be used to make things happen:

- Resource power: the control of things like money, property and information.
- Position power: the power or authority to make decisions or issue instructions.
- Expert power: the possession of particular knowledge and skills.

In the past, says Handy, resource power tended to dominate, but as organisations became larger and more complex, the bias swung towards position power. Now, it is expert power which is often the most influential and the most acceptable. People with the knowledge and skills which are needed to get things done can be more influential than the manager who tries to rely on position power. He or she may think they can rely on their formal authority, but if their objectives depend for their achievement on the application of special know-how, it is really the specialist who rules the roost.

In a local authority setting, it may be thought that Handy underestimates the continued importance of resource power. Most managers could quote examples of the director of finance who can mysteriously find the funds for one project but not for another – although this, perhaps, is a combination of resource and expert power. Control of information has also been a potent source of power, though the development of common databases is undermining the ability of some managers to use their ownership of information to boost or protect their scope for influencing things.

Position power – 'do it because I am the manager and I say so' – is certainly of decreasing if not discredited influence. People are less ready to be bossed about in this way. More importantly, many local authority activities have become far too complex for any one manager to have an adequate grasp of all the technicalities involved. Falling back on the right to give orders is often a sign of managerial weakness. The challenge is to co-ordinate and motivate an array of expert inputs, each of which may have the power (through specialist expertise) to change the direction of an initiative.

This illustrates Handy's fourth type of influence – negative power. "Even the humblest of us", says Handy, "can stop something, even if we can't start anything". In too many local authorities it would be easy to find examples of where expert power has been used negatively. Personnel departments once had the reputation of being the place to go to be told what you could not do. Some lawyers are far better at advising against action than in using ingenuity and initiative to find helpful loopholes in the law. And both resource and position power can also be used negatively.

Most managers, as Handy points out, have to make do formally with whatever resources and position they have been allocated. There are limits, too, to how much expert power any one person can exercise – it is impossible to be an expert in everything. So what can anyone do to increase their power position? Handy suggests:

- Increase position power by having friends in the right places – so tapping into other people's power. Establish a power base.
- Increase resource power by building alliances with other departments. Use other people's resources on a trading or barter basis.

- Increase resource power, also, by collecting information. Become known as a source of useful information which is not readily available elsewhere.
- Diminish other people's negative power by accepting compromise.

We all have to play politics, says Handy, but provided this is not carried to extremes it is not necessarily a bad thing. The skilful use of influence is how many excellent initiatives take off.

Meredith Belbin on winning teams

Dr Meredith Belbin is recognised, at least in the UK, as a leading guru of teams and team-building. Many local government managers have completed the Belbin team-role questionnaire and been told which of his nine team types they most resemble. Most of Belbin's ideas about teams originated from his studies of groups of managers undertaking team tasks on management courses at the Henley Administrative Staff College (now just Henley College). To Belbin's initial surprise, teams whose members were selected from the intellectually brightest members of the courses tended to perform very badly. Within these teams of very clever people, endless time was spent in abortive argument, no-one was ready to abandon their own views, each had a flair for spotting flaws in the others' arguments. Nothing actually got done. This led Belbin to study what made teams work badly or well, and led to the conclusion that what was needed was a blend of several different types of team member.

Team working is becoming increasingly important in local authorities as more and more issues cut across traditional professional or departmental boundaries, and as a range of expertise has to be deployed to address ever more complex issues. An understanding of how the choice of personalities for team membership can affect a team's effectiveness is consequently of considerable value. Belbin has suggested that a winning team has the following characteristics:

- A team leader who is a natural co-ordinator. A patient person who the others trust. Not domineering, but able to pull things together when a decision is needed. They need a good level of intelligence but need not be the most intellectually able member of the team.
- At least one 'Plant'. A Plant, in Belbin's typology is someone who is creative and imaginative, good at solving problems, may be unorthodox but is very bright and has lots of ideas.
- A fair spread of mental abilities. If everyone in the team is an intellectual genius they will all compete instead of collaborate. This does not imply that teams need dim people, but some modestly intellectual though practical personalities are a useful balance to the very bright Plants.
- A spread of team types. Most teams benefit from having a variety of personalities including, in Belbin's terminology and in addition to co-ordinators and plants:
  — 'resource investigators': extrovert enthusiasts who explore opportunities and make useful contacts;
  — 'shapers': dynamic, let's-get-on-with-it types who challenge, pressurise and find ways round obstacles;

— 'monitor-evaluators': serious types who can make cool, balanced judgements;
— 'teamworkers': sociable, helpful, perceptive people who can reduce friction;
— 'implementers': reliable and practically-minded types, concerned with efficiency and getting things done;
— 'completers': the conscientious, painstaking types who identify errors and omissions;
— 'specialists': the single-minded experts.
Belbin does not suggest that every winning team needs every type. The best spread of types depends on the type of task the team is working on, but he does argue that the effective team needs a spread.

- A match between team members' individual team aptitudes and the roles they are given in the team. So if the team needs someone to explore possible sources of help or resources from elsewhere, this should be given to the person whose personality fits the resource-investigator type. And a completer would make a terrible team leader.
- Self-knowledge within the team of the theory of team typology and team processes. Belbin suggests that teams which are aware of the different contribution which the various team types can make, and are able to identify strengths and weaknesses in their composition, are able to adjust the way they work to compensate for any shortfalls.

In real life, unlike at management college, it is rarely possible to select the membership of a team on the basis of an analysis of team personality types. But local authorities which use the Belbin concept are able to make better choices of team members when a degree of choice is open. They stand a much better chance of avoiding the not uncommon team failures caused by all the members being specialists or completers (in Belbin's meaning of the words) than authorities which select team members simply for their specialist knowledge or attention to detail.

Without comment

The following is a miscellany of short quotes from various gurus which seem to have some relevance to the hard-pressed local authority chief executive or manager who still has the motivation to strive do the right things better, and is committed to continuous self-development.

"The most common source of mistakes in management decisions is the emphasis on finding the right answer rather than the right question".
(Peter Drucker in *The Practice of Management*)

"The leaders who work most effectively, it seems to me, never say 'I... They don't think 'I'. They think 'we': they think 'team'."
(Peter Drucker in *Managing the Non-Profit Organisation*)

"The degree to which the opportunity to use power effectively is granted to or withheld from individuals is one operative difference between those companies which stagnate and those which innovate".
(Rosabeth Moss Kanter in *The Change Masters*)

"Learning is not finding out what other people already know, but a process of solving our own problems".
(Charles Handy in *Inside Organisations*)

"Our problem is not learning new things per se: it is letting go of what we know. It is managing the 'forgetting curve' as well as the learning curve".
(CK Prahalad in an article in *People Management*)

"Give the workforce a chance to work with pride and the 3% that apparently don't care will erode itself by peer pressure".
(W Edwards Deming in *Out of the Crisis*)

"Maintain one good friend who revels in telling you that you're full of hooey".
(Tom Peters in *The Pursuit of Wow*)

"Celebrate – formally and informally – the small wins that are indicative of the solid day-to-day performance turned in by 90% of your workforce".
(Tom Peters in *Thriving on Chaos*)

"Dividing an elephant in half does not make two small elephants".
(Peter Senge in *The Fifth Discipline*)

"When our thinking about quality expands to consider losses to society and quality audits of everything from nuts to soup in the canteen we are on the right track".
(Richard Schonberger in *Building a Chain of Customers*)

"As few people as possible should be involved in the performance of a process".
(Michael Hammer and James Champy in *Re-engineering the Corporation*)

"Free time is made, not found, in the manager's job: it is forced into the schedule. Hoping to leave some time open for contemplation or planning is tantamount to hoping the pressures of the job will go away".
(Henry Mintzberg in *Mintzberg on Management*)

"Most of the time senior managers should not be formulating strategy at all: they should be getting on with making their organisations as effective as possible in pursuing the strategies they already have".
(Henry Mintzberg in *Mintzberg on Management*)

"Fortune is the arbiter of half the things we do, leaving the other half or so to be controlled by ourselves... A wise prince should never take things easy in times of peace, but rather use the latter assiduously in order to reap the profit in times of adversity".
(Machiavelli in *The Prince*)

"We must shift the whole basis of leadership, motivation and administration towards the encouragement of the individual and away from the bureaucratic treatment of groups".
(Sir John Harvey-Jones in *All Together Now*)

"Management is about... maintaining the highest rate of change that the organisation and the people within it can stand".
(Sir John Harvey-Jones in *Managing to Survive*)

Footnotes:
1. *People and Performance*, Peter Drucker, Butterworth Heinemann, 1977.
2. *The Pursuit of Wow*, Tom Peters, Macmillan, 1995.
3. *ibid.*
4. *All Together Now*, Sir John Harvey-Jones, Heinemann,1994.
5. *Career Anchors*, Edgar Schein, Pfeiffer, 1990.
6. *Inside Organisations*, Charles Handy, BBC Books, 1990.
7. *Management Teams*, R Meredith Belbin, Butterworth Heinemann, 1981.

A note on further reading

Managers whose interest has been caught by any of the ideas and quotations in this book can delve more deeply into the topics involved by reading any of the books listed at the end of each chapter.

But many managers have too little time for what is often very solid reading – particularly of those books by American gurus which sometimes give the impression of being designed to be sold by weight. For example, the hardback edition of Tom Peters' *Thriving on Chaos* has 560 pages and Peter Senge's *The Fifth Discipline,* 413. British authors are far more economical in their use of words (and paper), with Charles Handy's *Age of Unreason* and *Inside Organisation*, and Sir John Harvey-Jones *All Together Now* all weighing in at only just over 200 pages each.

For managers who want to widen their knowledge of what the gurus say without reading even the shorter UK authors, there are three excellent British books which provide easy-reference guides to the key concepts of a very wide range of management thinkers.

- *Guide to the Management Gurus* by Carol Kennedy (Century Business, 1991) gives potted outlines of the ideas of 34 influential management gurus.
- *Managing with the Gurus* also by Carol Kennedy (Century Business, 1994) summarises the gurus' thinking about 20 management concepts and techniques.
- *Key Management Ideas* by Stuart Crainer (Pitman Publishing, 1996) looks at some two dozen management topics, summarising and commenting on the contribution to the concepts involved of some 60 management gurus.